Funny Shorts

15 short plays

Billy Aronson

D0927526

BROADWAY PLAY PUBLISHING INC
224 E 62nd St, NY NY 10065-8201
212 772-8334 fax: 212 772-8358
BroadwayPlayPubl.com

First printing: December 2014
Second printing: February 2015
I S B N: 978-0-88145-603-5

Book design: Marie Donovan
Page make-up: Adobe InDesign
Typeface: Palatino
Printed and bound in the U S A

CONTENTS

About the Author..*iv*

Thanks...*v*

REUNIONS..1

THE NEWS 17

LITTLE DUCK...31

IN THE MIDDLE OF THE NIGHT 57

NIGHT RULES 71

LIGHT YEARS...85

LITTLE RED RIDING HOOD 109

NEGOTIATION 129

GUILT 137

BLEEP THIS BLEEP...149

OF TWO MINDS...171

BEATLES FOREVER...203

AT THE BEACH...221

FREE WILL..233

COMPLETE UNKNOWNS 273

ABOUT THE AUTHOR

Billy Aronson's one-act plays have been produced in 8 Ensemble Studio Theatre Marathons and published in 6 volumes of *Best American Short Plays*. His full-length plays have premiered at Playwrights Horizons, the Woolly Mammoth, the San Francisco Playhouse, and 1812 Productions. His writing for the musical theater includes the original concept and additional lyrics for the Broadway musical RENT, and the book for the Theatreworks musical CLICK CLACK MOO. With artist Jennifer Oxley he created *Peg + Cat*, an animated P B S show that won 3 Emmy Awards in its first season. With his wife Lisa Vogel he created Jake and Anna, their animated offspring. "www.BillyAronson. com"

THANKS

Thanks to my parents, Willard Aronson and Joanne Morgan, for loving the performing arts and sharing that love with me. Thanks to my sister Dorothy and brother Joe, for being in those plays I made up when I was 7 and they were 5 and 3.

Thanks to my wife Lisa Vogel and our kids Jake and Anna, who are a part of all of these plays and everything I do.

Thanks to my teachers Virginia Clater, Joan Cobb, Carol MacVey, Alan MacVey, Michael Goldman, Larry Kornfeld, Oscar Brownstein, and Richard Gilman.

Thanks to the Ensemble Studio Theatre Marathon, the annual one-act play festival where many of these plays premiered.

Thanks to the actors, directors, producers, designers, composers, and the audiences of initial productions of the plays, all of whom collaborated in their creation.

Thanks to you for reading them, and being a part of my work in this way.

—Billy Aronson

REUNIONS

REUNIONS had its world premiere in Marathon 2002 at the Ensemble Studio Theatre's (Curt Dempster, Artistic Director). The cast and creative contributors were:

TABBY ECKERSLY .... Hope Chernov
SARAH BURKE NELSON/
CONNIE CUMMINGS........ .... Katherine Leask
ALAN ROADS/BRANDON TAVELLE .... Thomas Lyons
RICK ARZOOMANIAN .... Grant Shaud
NANCY MCCANN .... Maria Gabriele

Director .... Jamie Richards
Lighting .... Greg MacPherson
Set. .... Jennifer Varbalow
Costumes .... Leslie Bernstein
Sound .... Rob Gould
Props .... Ilene Weintraub

CHARACTERS

TABBY ECKERSLY, *is an independent publisher.*

SARAH BURK NELSON, *is a mother.*

ALAN ROADS, *doesn't know what he is.*

RICK ARZOOMANIAN, *is a pirate.*

NANCY MCCANN, *is a giraffe.*

CONNIE CUMMINGS, *is Santa Claus.*

BRANDON TAVELLE, *is a warlock.*

(ALAN, SARAH, *and* TABBY *stand there talking.*)

TABBY: Because in publishing the manuscript is everything, if you don't like the manuscript I mean that's all you've got, it's your life.

SARAH: Sure.

TABBY: And I was getting manuscripts that, well some of them were fine but I couldn't get behind them, not with every bone in my body.

SARAH: Uh huh.

TABBY: And then one day I just woke up and it was clear as day that I had to just go ahead on my own.

SARAH: You're your own boss, that's so great.

TABBY: I have complete control, every single manuscript I believe in with every bone in my body, every fiber.

ALAN: I taught high school for eleven years! Then I quit and sold computers! Now I'm back in graduate school!

SARAH: I can't believe it's been nine years since I had a job.

TABBY: But you're a mom. That's so great.

SARAH: It's amazing, watching them figure stuff out, you learn so much.

TABBY: That's what everybody says.

SARAH: They're born with these real personalities, then they grow into these people that you really like, they're your pals, this whole team just came out of your body.

TABBY: It must be amazing.

SARAH: They can get you so angry, you never knew you could be so angry, or so in love, in whole new ways.

TABBY: I've really got to do that when I meet the right person.

SARAH: It's worth waiting for the right person.

ALAN: I keep meeting the right person but I can never convince her that I'm the right person!

TABBY: Now that I'm in control of my work it'll be easier.

ALAN: Let's head to the tent! There's going to be dancing!

SARAH: If I leave Bob with the kids one more minute he'll kill me.

TABBY: Has anybody seen Donna Cunningham? We said we'd share a table.

SARAH: Did you hear Connie Cummings is going to be here?

TABBY: Connie Cummings, really?, I can't believe it.

SARAH: My kids are dying to meet her.

TABBY: When I tell people I went to school with Connie Cummings they think I'm making it up.—Hey is that Rick Arzoomanian? *(To off)* Rick. Rick.

(RICK enters. He's a pirate.)

TABBY: Tabby Eckersly. Remember?

RICK: Hey Tabby.

TABBY: Did you know Sarah Burk?

SARAH: Sarah Burk Nelson.

RICK: Sarah, sure.

ALAN: I'm Alan Roads! I was friends with Gary Fine!

RICK: Hey Alan.

TABBY: I read that you were a pirate in the paper, that's so great.

SARAH: Really.

RICK: I was getting nowhere on land. Just knocking on doors, year after year. So I put together a crew and headed out to sea.

TABBY: You just did it.

SARAH: That's so great.

RICK: It was tough out there for a while. There was nothing happening and the sun was killing us.

TABBY: Sure.

RICK: But then I saw this ship and I felt that it was ready for new ownership.

TABBY: You just had a feeling.

RICK: I felt the time was right and this was my chance. So I set my sights and I went for it with everything I had.

TABBY: Wow.

SARAH: I read about this.

RICK: It was a real battle, it was tougher than I thought. It cost me this eye, but we kept on fighting and we did it.

TABBY: That's something.

RICK: We pulled a real coup, and when I opened the treasure there were rubies and sapphires and diamonds packed together so tight. And just like that we went from struggling to stay afloat to being a major player on the sea.

TABBY: I'd been reading manuscripts that meant nothing to me, well some were okay but I couldn't get behind them so one morning I just woke up and decided to go independent and now it's great.

SARAH: I've missed working but you can't believe the way kids are born with these real personalities, you've got this whole team of people you love.

ALAN: I got sick of teaching so I went into sales and now I'm back in school!

RICK: Has anyone seen Chris Dumars?

SARAH: Are you in touch with Chris?

RICK: I haven't seen Dumars in years.

TABBY: Did you hear Connie Cummings is going to be here?

RICK: I heard she might.

ALAN: Let's head to the tent for the dancing!

TABBY: I was going to wait for Donna Cunningham and get a table.

SARAH: I've really got to get back to Bob and the kids or he'll kill me. *(She goes.)*

TABBY: But to have all that treasure, right at your feet, all of a sudden.

RICK: I felt shocked, and I felt proud.

TABBY: Now that I'm finally working on manuscripts I really believe in it's so liberating.

RICK: There were emeralds and sapphires and rubies—

ALAN: Guess I'll head to the tent! *(He goes.)*

TABBY: And didn't it totally make up for all the years, you know all the knocking on doors?

RICK: I had this feeling for the first time that I really was a pirate. I wasn't just pretending or going through the motions.

TABBY: At first I'd look down at these manuscripts and I couldn't believe I'm really attached to such brave and honest material that I can totally pour myself into.

RICK: We're a major player and heat isn't a problem, and we don't have to worry about the wind.

TABBY: My brain isn't chained to this garbage that I can't really get behind, I kept telling myself it would happen but it really has happened.

RICK: And I feel like this is just where I should be right now. And I'm headed exactly where I should be headed.

TABBY: Donna Cunningham's supposed to be here, we're going to get a table, you should join us.

RICK: That would be good.

TABBY: *(To off)* Donna, is that you? Donna.

(NANCY enters. She's a giraffe.)

TABBY: Nancy McCann. I'm sorry. I thought that you were Donna Cunningham.

RICK: Nancy. Hi.

TABBY: So you're a giraffe.

(RICK and TABBY look at NANCY. NANCY looks at them.)

RICK: That's Donna Cunningham over there.

TABBY: *(To off)* Donna, it's me Tabby. Do you have an extra seat for Rick Arzoomanian? *(To Rick)* She has an extra seat, you should join us.

RICK: That would be good. Except…is that Rich Kravitz at her table?

TABBY: Rich Kravitz and Donna used to go out.

RICK: I don't feel like sitting yet.

TABBY: But wouldn't you have a lot to say to Rich since he's a pirate too?

RICK: I think I'll stay here.

TABBY: He's a really successful pirate, you know that right, from the papers?

RICK: I don't read the papers.

TABBY: He was on magazines too, and T V for months.

RICK: I'll stay here and see who's around.

TABBY: You're sure?

RICK: I'll stay here I think.

TABBY: I really have to say hi to Donna.

RICK: Okay. I'll be here.

TABBY: Okay.

(TABBY *goes.* RICK *talks to* NANCY.)

RICK: It was a real battle all right, it cost me this eye. But we hung in there and we did it, and when I got to the treasure there were rubies and there were sapphires packed in there so tight. And there were diamonds, and now we're a major force on the sea. We're smaller than some. We're a small major force. So we're not so widely recognized. But we're expanding. *(To off)* Connie Cummings. Connie.

(CONNIE *enters. She's Santa Claus.)*

CONNIE: *(To Rick)* Stuart Beamish? Oh hi.

RICK: Rick Arzoomanian. Remember?

CONNIE: Rick, so you're a pirate, and Nancy you're a giraffe, what great things to be.

RICK: I'm a pirate all right, Connie.

CONNIE: It's a terrific time to be a pirate. And to be a giraffe.

RICK: And you're Santa Claus.

CONNIE: It's strange sometimes, to actually be the real Santa.

RICK: Sure.

CONNIE: To really be based in the North Pole. To actually fly the whole globe in one night.

RICK: It must be something.

CONNIE: Everybody makes a big deal about how I'm the first woman Santa and that's great, what it says to girls and what it means.

RICK: Sure.

CONNIE: But on a day to day basis it's much more about dealing with the media. Protecting the image, making it fresh for a new millennium.

RICK: Sure.

CONNIE: The elves handle construction pretty much on their own but you have to keep an eye on that, and deal with reindeer unions.

RICK: Uh huh.

CONNIE: But when winter rolls around it's still about the joy, bringing joy to the world.

RICK: I'd been getting nowhere on land, year after year.

CONNIE: Uh huh.

RICK: So I got a crew together and headed to sea and I saw this ship, and I had a feeling, that it was ready for new ownership and so we took it on and—

CONNIE: Uh huh.

RICK: —and when I opened the treasure I saw, there was—

(BRANDON *enters. He's a warlock.*)

BRANDON: Connie Cummings. Brandon Tavelle.
Remember?

CONNIE: So you're a witch.

BRANDON: (*Wounded*) I'm not a witch, I'm a warlock.

CONNIE: What a great thing to be, Brandon.

BRANDON: Always knew I had something. Through
all the crap I endured. The winking and whispering
at those cliquey drinking parties. Anthony Oaks and
Sally Bottini. Or Little Miss Muppet and her brainless
cronies in the back of the lecture hall saving four seats
with an apple so they could point at me and giggle. Or
the marching-band-lacrosse-gang with their esoteric
handshakes and midnight sing-songs which they
always topped off with the obligatory run down the
hallway to howl their lewd nicknames and puke in
my shoes. I wanted to jump off the tower, but I buried
myself in the library, found this book about spells and
my god that was me. I could pull toads out of people's
ears. I could turn those toads into snakes, and make
the snakes disappear in a burst of flame. I knew I could
do it, and now: I do. And it has this affect. A power.
Not just on my parents. Total strangers come up to
me, with this look, you can see it. They open their
mouths, not a damn sound comes out, because they're
speechless.

CONNIE: It's a terrific time to be in witchcraft.

BRANDON: (*Destroyed*) I'm not a witch. I'm a warlock.
(*He storms off.*)

RICK: And when I opened the treasure there were
rubies. And sapphires. And diamonds. And they were
all packed in there so tight.

CONNIE: Huh.

RICK: Emeralds and rubies, and silver, there was silver in there. And I felt shocked and I felt proud, and so lucky, that it was all right there, all at once. Everything I needed was right at my feet, we'd gone from struggling to stay afloat to being a major force. And now the heat doesn't bother us, and the wind is no problem. We're going in just the right direction as a major force on the sea.

CONNIE: When I go flying on Christmas eve I go down the chimney of everybody, every person on earth, rich and poor, every nation, from home to home to home it's such a rush as you get going, you get into this rhythm and it's intoxicating.

RICK: It must be.

CONNIE: To make their lives so full and so special with these things they've been dying for all year, things they want and they need that are thrilling and wholesome, pure joy that's really good for them, electric and lasting and real.

RICK: That's something.

CONNIE: To drop off their dreams and head back to the sky and hear billions of people gasping and screaming your name, can you imagine?, giving intensely personal perfect pleasure to every human being on earth and having that be your job?, it's not even a job it's a privilege, I'm tremendously fortunate to be able to make life on earth worth living and bring the entire planet to this state of indescribable ecstasy again and again there's nothing like it.

RICK: Huh.

CONNIE: And the next day and the next to see entire families still caught in the glow of this golden moment and know you've lifted their hearts and brought a sense of hope and dignity and given them the strength to grow and really reach for their dreams and to feel in your gut that every chimney you went down was completely worthwhile.

RICK: M.

CONNIE: The stockings hung with glee for godsake, and the cookies and milk by the fireplace, and the songs all over the radio and T V specials on every network with every major pop star they can drag out singing your praise and the drawings, entire kindergarten classes doing drawings and collages and plays and your picture's on their lunch boxes I mean couldn't you die?

(RICK *nods.*)

CONNIE: There's nothing else I could stand for three seconds after this, any other work would be torture because absolutely nothing else gives such undisputed pleasure with total universal recognition and I'm so ridiculously lucky to be doing exactly what I'm doing I could laugh every second of my blest and spectacular life. *(To off)* Hey Stuart Beamish. It's me. Connie Cummings. I'm fucking Santa Claus.

(CONNIE *goes.* RICK *gasps for breath, staggers, fists clenched, suffocating.*)

RICK: She's lucky all right. Her uncle was Santa Claus. Like that didn't help. If my uncle was Santa Claus I'd be handing out presents. But my uncle wasn't Santa Claus. I was on my own. Knocking on doors. Dying in the heat. Til I saw that ship. And there was rubies. And silver. And diamonds. Where's Chris Dumars.

(RICK *staggers away, falls, crawls off.* NANCY *stands there.* TABBY *runs on, laughing and sobbing hysterically.*)

TABBY: Oh Nancy hi, did you know Donna Cunningham is pregnant, it's so great, they'd been trying for so long, and she's got this great guy, he gets along great with her friends, and Rich Kravitz has these adorable girls and the sweetest wife, and Sarah Burk's about to have her fourth, and Bob is such a great dad, and I'm finally working on manuscripts that really mean something to me, they're new and beautiful and fresh and so strong I can go out and push with every muscle in my body, every cell, all my blood and my skin and my guts and my soul.

(TABBY *runs off.* NANCY *stands there.* ALAN *enters stepping carefully, struggling for balance.*)

ALAN: Nancy McCann! I'm Alan Roads! I was in your freshman comp! You wrote such great papers! I used to follow you across the green! Gary Fine and Gary Bowman said I should stop stalking you and ask you out! Meanwhile I didn't know Gary and Gary were going out with each other! I sure wish they were here now but they're dead! All my friends are gone and I have nothing to say and no idea what I'm doing! Hey the music's starting, let's dance Nancy McCann! You had great ideas and now your head's way up in the trees and I'm still down here, but I'd feel way up there if you'd dance with me! So let's dance, Nancy McCann!.

(*A pop tune from years ago plays, such as* We Are Family. ALAN *holds on to* NANCY. ALAN *and* NANCY *begin to dance.* RICK *and* TABBY *enter dancing together.*)

(*At first the dancing is self-conscious.* ALAN *and* NANCY *are timid and reserved.* RICK *and* TABBY *dance cautiously, carefully showing off to one another. But as they continue to dance, both couples let go, become more expressive, joyous, and free.* CONNIE *joins the dancing, as do* BRANDON, *and* SARAH.)

END OF PLAY

THE NEWS

Stage production rights licensed by Playscripts Inc.

THE NEWS was originally produced by Ensemble Studio Theatre's L A Project (Michael C Mahon & Laura Jane Salvato, Artistic Directors). The cast and creative contributors were:

HILLARY ....Jacqueline Wright
KAREN ....Liz Ross
DAVID...Ray Xifo
GEORGE ....Hiram Kasten

Director...Lisa James

THE NEWS received its New York premiere in Marathon 2007 at Ensemble Studio Theatre's (William Carden, Artistic Director). The cast and creative contributors were:

HILLARY .... Diana Ruppe
KAREN .... Geneva Carr
DAVID..Thomas Lyons
GEORGE .... Grant Shaud

Director..Jamie Richards
Costumes...Amela Baksic
Set ....Ryan Elliot Kravetz
Lighting.. Evan Purcell
Props .... Amanda J Haley
Sound ....Ryan Maeker

CHARACTERS

HILLARY
KAREN
DAVID
GEORGE

(*A hospital bed and two chairs.* KAREN *sits in the bed wearing a smock.* HILLARY *sits in a chair wearing a suit and holding a wrapped bouquet.*)

HILLARY: So the thing, is still there.

KAREN: They decided not to take it out at the last minute, I had symptoms that didn't add up so they did a test and they found something else.

HILLARY: So when will they, take out this other thing.

KAREN: Well they can't because of where it is and how far it is along.

HILLARY: But I don't see why they don't get the first thing. They said they could just go in and get it, the sooner the better.

KAREN: There's no point in going in there because this new thing's a lot further along.

(HILLARY *starts to cry.*)

KAREN: I'm not crying because tears don't help.

(HILLARY *struggles not to cry.*)

KAREN: There are things they can give me and methods that might slow things down. I'm going to make every choice with my eyes open just like I've been doing from day one, I've been getting the name of every doctor and every hallway otherwise you run the risk of waking up in the dark with no idea why parts of you are numb and all these smells are coming out of you.

(KAREN's *cell phone rings—a soft, simple tone. She checks it, touches a button to stop the ringing.*)

KAREN: I'm only taking it if it's George which it's
not because he thinks I'm in the operating room 'til
four, he doesn't know they did the test. You thought I
was supposed to be out of the operating room at two
because that was the original plan but they pushed it
back to four and I forgot to tell people but it's good you
came early after all. Talk to me about work.

HILLARY: It's okay.

KAREN: I can't wait to get back, you have no idea about
these new drugs, or maybe I could work from home,
there are side effects but it's a trade-off like the ones
I'm on now.

(HILLARY's phone rings—a soft, simple tone different from
KAREN's. She touches a button to stop the ringing.)

HILLARY: I'm sorry I'll turn it off—

KAREN: Leave it on. Sound is good. Maybe I should call
George but he's at work, he really has to get caught up
and he'll be here soon anyway. The only other call I'd
take would be Abigail who's on a trip with her choir, I
said she should go.

HILLARY: How is she.

KAREN: She's fine. She's a fine child. She's her own
person. She's become her own person and I love the
person she's become. She expresses herself. She makes
her own decisions. She's so aware of the world and her
position in it. How did it happen so fast, she's only ten
years old, do you realize that?, but you can already see
the person she's become, and I'm so proud of that little
girl, I adore her so much.

HILLARY: (Nods) Mmm.

KAREN: We had some hard times, she and I. She didn't
like me for a while. But it turns out the reason she
didn't like me is because she thought I didn't like her.
Imagine that. But now she knows I really like her and

she likes me again. *(Beat.)* The thing is to do what you can, that's the challenge, if you want to jog you jog or there are machines, or if you want to go to the movies then you just do it and people understand and if you can't sit there or there's trouble controlling the muscles in your face at a restaurant or if there are sounds that you're making people accept that, or if you're embarrassed you can pace yourself or go home if you have to and there are tricks you can learn, like if your balance tilts you can compensate or if things spin or there's a shaking in your chin you can compensate or if it stings when you press down your foot.

(KAREN's phone rings. She checks it, touches a button to stop the ringing.)

KAREN: But the thing is to keep going because everybody's working within a clock, nobody knows it but we all have a different clock and you can't possibly know what it says so the thing is to get in as many meaningful moments with people who mean something to you, a meaningful moment just happens in a time and a place, planning doesn't help, you can organize all you want but then nothing happens but then something just presents itself and you try to enjoy it.

HILLARY: You mean so much to me, Karen.

KAREN: Well sure we mean a lot to each other, all of us, we've done so much and we appreciate each other and what we've done. And of course we've been angry, we've had these tensions but that comes from trying to accomplish what's best for us all which we each try to do in our individual ways so of course there's frustration but of course we forgive without even explaining because there just isn't time for it all.

HILLARY: Sure.

KAREN: It's so important, to just, to stop with the, I really need to just do what I, you know, to get out, and go to the beach. Sunshine. The sound of water. To look out at all that water. To feel the wind and the sunshine on your arms and hear the water and people talking, and laughing. There's laughing. And you can join right in with the laughing. As long as you can breathe you can laugh.

(Pause. DAVID *enters wearing a suit, carrying a wrapped bouquet.)*

DAVID: Oh Karen, it must be so great to have it over. *(To* HILLARY*)* Hi.

HILLARY: Hi.

KAREN: They didn't take it out after all, they did another test and they found something else because I had these symptoms.

DAVID: Shit.

KAREN: There are treatments that can slow things down and I'll make my choices with my eyes open.

DAVID: Shit. Karen.

KAREN: I'm not cursing and I'm not crying I'm going to do what I can do.

DAVID: You need another opinion.

KAREN: What do you mean.

DAVID: People make mistakes. It happens all the time.

KAREN: I know they're right.

DAVID: Who told you? A specialist?

KAREN: My body told me.

DAVID: That's not a…what does George say.

KAREN: He's at work, he doesn't know about the test yet.

(HILLARY's *phone starts ringing.*)

DAVID: I'll talk to him. You're getting a second opinion, and you're joining a group. There are all kinds of groups. I'll help you find just the right group.

KAREN: A group of what.

DAVID: You know, people who know all about your situation.

KAREN: I should get into, a situation?

(HILLARY *touches a button to stop the ringing.*)

DAVID: I mean a group of people who understand what you're going through. You can just open up, believe me, it's an opportunity. We're all so covered up. We have to be, to get by. But they have ways to help you let everything go. And these bonds develop, these wonderful bonds, and there's a whole new quality. What exactly did they tell you. Was the person a specialist? What exactly did they say.

KAREN: When they prick your arm to knock you out there's a flash where you're fifteen and you're standing at the sink and there's a twitch in a part of you that you didn't know you had but when you touch it it's crawling away. *(Pause)* What's it like out.

HILLARY: It's nice.

KAREN: They said it was going to rain.

HILLARY: It cleared up.

DAVID: They don't give you anything to put flowers in. I'll round something up. *(He starts to go.)*

KAREN: Sit. Bodies in the room is good.

(DAVID *sits. Pause.* GEORGE *enters, wearing a suit, carrying as many balloons as he can hold.*)

GEORGE: You're supposed to be in the operating room.

KAREN: I thought you were working.

GEORGE: I got halfway there and it hit me I should have balloons in your room when you got out.

(DAVID *and* HILLARY *stand.*)

KAREN: Sit.

DAVID: We can walk around while you guys talk.

KAREN: Sit down.

(DAVID *and* HILLARY *sit.* DAVID'*s phone rings—an elaborate tone. He touches a button to stop the ringing.*)

KAREN: Leave it on.

GEORGE: These balloons are wet. How did they get wet. Something happened to these balloons to make them wet. Okay. Specks on the sidewalk. It rained for a few seconds. That's right. It rained. But that was before I bought the balloons. So that's not it. Oh wait. My hip is sore. I was lying on the back of a car. A car backed into me as I crossed the street. I was in the middle of the intersection on the back of a car. People were shouting are you all right. So the balloons got wet from the back windshield. Except they were still in the bag, and the bag wasn't opened, so that's not it. Wait, wait. When I came out of the elevator I ran right into a guy who had a cup of soda that he probably spilled all over. But it was cola, and the droplets on the balloons are clear. So maybe I went back out and it rained again. Or maybe the ceiling leaks. Or maybe the balloons are sweating.

(GEORGE'*s cell phone rings—a soft, simple tone, different from* HILLARY'*s and* KAREN'*s. He ignores it, drops the balloons.*)

KAREN: Don't leave them on the floor if they're wet.

GEORGE: Hi.

DAVID: Hi.

HILLARY: Hi.

KAREN: My friends are here because I didn't tell them the operation got pushed back.

GEORGE: They're always changing things here and I'm sick of it.

KAREN: They decided not to operate after all because they ran another test.

GEORGE: I could have gotten you the best doctor in the world if you could have just been ready one day sooner.

KAREN: This hospital has the best reputation in the world.

GEORGE: What does a reputation do?, nothing. I could have gotten you the number one guy.

KAREN: The doctors here are the best anywhere.

GEORGE: They're not number one. The number one guy is in Europe by now.

KAREN: Could you pick up the balloons?

GEORGE: I'll blow up the last one so you can see the whole effect.

KAREN: Pick up the balloons and sit down 'cause we have to talk.

(GEORGE *tries to blow up the last balloon. He's out of breath, so it's difficult, noisy and messy.*)

GEORGE: Fuck. (*He stretches the balloon again and again, tries to blow it up again, finally fills it up. Then he tries to tie it, but his fingers are weak and shaky so it's a struggle. Unable to tie the balloon, he finally lets it go; it shoots away in all directions.*)

KAREN: Pick up the balloons.

GEORGE: You can't talk to me like that.

KAREN: I've said it every other way.

GEORGE: You can't use that tone on me.

KAREN: I'll say what I have to say in the way I need to say it to be heard.

GEORGE: If you want me to hear you, you can't use that tone.

KAREN: I don't want the floor to be slippery and the balloons bother me down there.

GEORGE: Please explain how balloons on the floor is more disturbing than phones ringing.

KAREN: I just wasn't expecting balloons.

GEORGE: At your surprise party you said they made all the difference.

KAREN: That was for Abigail's party and she was six.

GEORGE: It was for your birthday and you said they made all the difference.

KAREN: It was for Abigail.

GEORGE: It was for you, it was your surprise party.

KAREN: If you keep saying it does that make it true?

GEORGE: I don't even hear you when you use that tone.

KAREN: Do you realize that you're yelling?

GEORGE: I don't even hear you when you use that tone.

KAREN: Do you realize you're yelling?

GEORGE: I don't hear what you're saying.

KAREN: You're yelling. Do you hear yourself?

GEORGE: You're the one who's yelling at me in front of your friends.

(DAVID *and* HILLARY *stand.*)

GEORGE & KAREN: Sit down.

(DAVID *and* HILLARY *sit.* HILLARY'*s phone rings once.*)

GEORGE: I'm sorry I didn't bring flowers like your friends but you used to love balloons.

KAREN: Please just get them off the—

GEORGE: *(Shouts)* I'm getting the balloons off the floor are you happy I'm getting them up even though there are no strings to hang them on and not one desk to put them on just like there are no vases here If this is the best hospital in the world oh I'd hate to see the worst hospital in the world I really would hate to see that Get up Get up up up.

(In a frenzy GEORGE bats the balloons up into the air. As they scatter he runs around the room to keep them up. GEORGE and KAREN break into laughter. They're laughing so hard they can hardly get the words out:)

GEORGE: The time with your uncle and the—

KAREN: Yeah—, yeah—

(Overwhelmed by laughter, KAREN flops back and GEORGE sinks to his knees. The laughter subsides.)

KAREN: I'm gonna miss you.

(GEORGE hides his head between his legs. KAREN covers her eyes with one hand. DAVID and HILLARY look away in different directions.)

(GEORGE rises, moves slowly towards KAREN.)

(GEORGE's phone rings. KAREN's phone rings. HILLARY's phone rings. DAVID's phone rings. All four phones ring, forming a strange chord that repeats in the rhythm of a heart beat, to provide a musical background for the rest of the play.)

GEORGE: You're coming home tonight?

KAREN: Do we still have the chicken?

GEORGE: I'll send out for chicken.

(DAVID *and* HILLARY *hold their bouquets in one hand, phones in the other, move closer to* GEORGE *and* KAREN, *sing softly into their phones as they observe.* GEORGE *and* KAREN *rub one another.*)

DAVID & HILLARY: They're having dinner at home.

KAREN: At our table? On our plates?

GEORGE: With our forks and our knives.

DAVID & HILLARY: They're having dinner at home.

KAREN: What's on T V?

GEORGE: Your show's on at nine.

KAREN: Is it a rerun?

GEORGE: It's a good one.

DAVID & HILLARY: They're watching T V.

KAREN: And then can we go for a walk?

GEORGE: Let's go for a walk.

DAVID & HILLARY: They're going for a walk.

(GEORGE *and* KAREN *put their hands together, rub one another's hands.*)

DAVID & HILLARY: They're holding hands.

END OF PLAY

LITTLE DUCK

LITTLE DUCK premiered in Marathon 2009 at Ensemble Studio Theatre's (William Carden, Artistic Director; Paul Alexander Slee, Executive Director). The cast and creative contributors were:

ROBERT .... Paul Bartholomew
HOLLY .... Jane Pfitsch
DR JILL .... Julie Leedes
R J .... Steven Boyer
ANNE .... Geneva Carr

Director .... Jamie Richards
Music composition .... Stephen Lawrence
Costumes .... Suzanne Chesney
Set .... Maiko Chii
Lighting .... Cat Tate
Props .... Joseph Heitman
Sound .... Shane Rettig

CHARACTERS

ROBERT, *the president*
HOLLY, *the intern*
ANNE, *the writer*
R J, *the artist*
DR JILL, *the director of content*

Scene 1. Robert and Holly

ROBERT: It's sweet and lovely but it's really smart, right, and funny?

HOLLY: It's so great, Robert.

ROBERT: And isn't it great that it's about how we can all work together and get along? Read me Darcy's note again?

HOLLY: "It's so sweet and funny and original, we at the network have the highest hopes for Little Duck."

ROBERT: The highest hopes.

HOLLY: She totally loves it.

ROBERT: She ordered a pilot and twelve episodes based on a ten page bible, when does that happen?

HOLLY: Have you heard from the people who helped with the bible?

ROBERT: They're all on board.

HOLLY: All of them?

ROBERT: R J'll do the designs, Anne'll be head writer, Doctor Jill'll be educational advisor and director of content.

HOLLY: Wow.

ROBERT: You'll give them total support. This takes priority over all your office duties.

HOLLY: Oh could I ask something about that?, one thing?, Cheryl said you said she could do the one-on-ones with the Little Duck people?

ROBERT: She'd asked about that a while ago.

HOLLY: Cheryl's so great, she's been a total friend, but to meet with those people one-on-one, to go back and forth between them and you about the creative stuff, that's like my dream.

ROBERT: Cheryl's been here longer.

HOLLY: I know and normally I wouldn't say anything but on this one project I think I could really contribute 'cause when I was reading your bible I totally felt the character, *(She demonstrates.)* how he waddles into the yard, taking in the day, dippin' his tail into the pond, feeling the cool droplets all tingly and sparkly in the sun, then stretching his feathers out as far as they'll go and givin' that little wet tail a shake-a-shake-a-shake. *(She shakes her tail.)*

ROBERT: You can do the one-on-ones with the Little Duck people.

(HOLLY yelps for joy.)

ROBERT: Cheryl won't like it. But this is Little Duck.

Scene 2. Doctor Jill and Anne

DR JILL: It's super. I just love it.

ANNE: Oh good.

DR JILL: I can't believe you turned a ten page bible into a totally fleshed out pilot script.

ANNE: It really worked for you?

DR JILL: It really gets the content across, and it's so funny.

ANNE: It's so hard getting characters to talk for the first time, plus there was all this pressure to impress Robert, and you.

DR JILL: With your resume I'm the one who should be nervous.

ANNE: Right. Anyway. Whew.

DR JILL: So can I show you my notes? They're mostly tiny.

ANNE: I want them, I need them.

DR JILL: Here you go.

ANNE: *(Reads)* Okay. Good. Good. You didn't like the jelly?

DR JILL: Kids might really do that at home.

ANNE: Okay. *(Reads)* Sure. Good.

DR JILL: The one other thing is, I think the pig should be physically challenged.

ANNE: The pig is a main character.

DR JILL: Uh huh.

ANNE: Did you run this by Robert?

DR JILL: Holly said he wants us to go ahead on our own, he'll take a look at what we come up with.

ANNE: The show is supposed to be funny.

DR JILL: Funny and sweet.

ANNE: I guess I, huh.

DR JILL: I know it's a big change, but kids who are physically challenged get so many clues that they should be hidden. In the way people avoid eye contact or withhold a greeting. This would put them front and center in a way that's really ground-breaking. So give it a try?

ANNE: But the thing is, the script has a balance between the characters, it's a pure complete thing, like a plant, you can't staple a nose on a flower, and what does that teach kids, that a message has to be forced, you see?

DR JILL: I guess when you talk about keeping the show pure I think of how in some societies undesirables were hidden away or even done away with, I know you're not saying that, but you see what I'm saying.

ANNE: No no, I know, but the thing about the Nazis was that in the name of their ideology they went around butchering people and lopping things off and squeezing things in where they didn't belong, so, yeah.

DR JILL: Anne. You've done so much great work. So let's see if we can't take it to the next step and make it really great. Okay?

ANNE: Sure. Anyway.

DR JILL: Okay then.

(DR JILL *goes to hug* ANNE, ANNE *gives* DR JILL *a violent shove.*)

DR JILL: Did you just—

ANNE: Weren't you about to—

DR JILL: I was going to hug you because—

ANNE: Sorry sorry, shit. Should we— (*Offers to hug*)

DR JILL: No no, that's okay.

ANNE: Okey doke.

Scene 3. Doctor Jill and R J

DR JILL: So you have this feeling, and your hand is drawing, and, are you thinking?

R J: Yeah.

DR JILL: You're thinking and feeling, and, do you have some idea what you're going for?

R J: I have a picture in my head.

DR JILL: A picture in your head. Wow. Does what comes out ever surprise you?

R J: Sure.

DR JILL: You're open to discovery, and out comes a new character who'll charm kids around the world and become part of their lives. Do you feel proud?

(R J shrugs.)

DR JILL: You should. You have a gift. Anyway, I had this idea that Little Pig should be physically challenged in some way. If you could do one of your amazing drawings it would be a huge help in getting the character approved.

(R J puts his hand on DR JILL's breast. She slaps him.)

DR JILL: You think because you're this young guy who's a big deal you can just put your hand on my breast? I should report you. Or pinch you, see how you like it. *(She pinches him.)* Do you like it when I pinch you? Do you?

R J: No.

DR JILL: I didn't hear you.

(DR JILL pinches R J again.)

R J: *(Louder)* No.

DR JILL: That's right you don't. Now give me that pig.

Scene 4. Anne and Holly

ANNE: Robert's meeting with Jill to go over the script before he's meeting with me?

HOLLY: Yeah.

ANNE: I'm the writer. So why's he going over the script with her first?

HOLLY: Well, I know he's really excited about this drawing of the pig R J did for Jill.

ANNE: R J did a drawing for Jill's idea?

HOLLY: Uh huh.

(ANNE *stands up, bites her fist, sits down.*)

ANNE: I need to be in that meeting with Robert and Jill.

HOLLY: Okay, Anne. I'll try and get you into that.

ANNE: Good. Thanks.

HOLLY: So since I'm doing this for you would you do one thing for me? —Now I feel weird asking you, ugh!, anyway I wrote this script for Little Duck and I know it's a total dream that it could ever get on the show but—oh god it's the first thing I ever wrote and you've been writing for T V longer than I've been alive but— ugh! ugh! —okay just go for it—could I show you my script?

ANNE: Of course.

HOLLY: (*Hands over script*) So what do you think?

ANNE: It looks good, Holly.

HOLLY: You're not laughing.

ANNE: I never laugh out loud at these things but—

HOLLY: You hate it, don't you.

ANNE: No I don't, it's really funny.

HOLLY: Where?

ANNE: Here *(Points to script, laughs)*, and here... *(Laughs and laughs)*

Scene 5. Robert, Anne, and Doctor Jill

(They nibble on cupcakes.)

DR JILL: Mm.

ANNE: Mm.

DR JILL: I love the ducks on top.

ROBERT: The feathers are coconut shavings.

ANNE: This one's cream-filled.

ROBERT: So how's everything going?

ANNE: Really well.

DR JILL: It's an amazing team.

ROBERT: Everybody working well with Holly?

ANNE: She's a pleasure.

DR JILL: How can she be so young and so sharp?

ROBERT: One day we'll all be working for Holly.

DR JILL/ANNE: I think so./Yeah.

ROBERT: Anyway, I love where you guys are going with the script.

ANNE: Oh good.

DR JILL: Anne's a wonderful writer.

ANNE: Jill's notes have been a big help.

DR JILL: It's easy when the material's so clear.

ROBERT: As far as the question about the jelly, let's just have it be mud.

DR JILL: Mud?

ROBERT: Yeah.

DR JILL: I wonder if that would encourage kids to bring mud into the house.

ROBERT: I don't think so.

ANNE: Mud is funny.

ROBERT: And I love the idea about having the pig be physically challenged.

DR JILL: Really?

ROBERT: It's so brave and original.

DR JILL: It means so much to me that you think that.

ANNE: I admire a lot about it, but I guess I wasn't sure how it would fit with what you created.

ROBERT: We have to be willing to change anything at any point to make the show great. I'm so proud of you, Jill.

DR JILL: Oh thanks, Robert.

ROBERT: I think it should be the raccoon though.

DR JILL: Little Duck's best friend should become a raccoon?

ROBERT: No, I'm talking about the raccoon character who visits the barn sometimes.

DR JILL: So we'd have a minor character be physically challenged?

ROBERT: I thought instead of physically challenged he'd be overweight.

ANNE: Interesting.

ROBERT: That's a problem kids deal with. They worry about it. They make fun of it. They don't understand.

DR JILL: Having it be the pig wouldn't work?

ROBERT: You can't have an overweight pig.

ANNE: You really can't.

DR JILL: Right. Oh yeah. But, the physically challenged major character, you didn't like?

ROBERT: It just doesn't feel Little Duck.

ANNE: It somehow doesn't.

DR JILL: I see what you mean, I guess.

ROBERT: We can get the overweight raccoon in the pilot, right Anne?

ANNE: Really?

ROBERT: I think we should.

ANNE: So much in the pilot is already set.

DR JILL: I have an idea for how to fit him in.

ANNE: I'll fit him in.

ROBERT: Great. It'll be great.

DR JILL: Definitely.

ANNE: It will.

ROBERT: You got coconut on your nose.

DR JILL: Oh thanks.

ANNE: I got gooped.

ROBERT: *(Eating)* Mm.

DR JILL: *(Eating)* Mm.

Scene 6. Anne and R J

(Words "in quotes" are screamed in a whisper.)

ANNE: It "fucking sucks", it makes "no fucking sense", the instant he said it I thought what the "fuck is he talking about" but I acted like I liked it because I'm a "fucked up piece of fucking shit." Anyway, I don't know how you feel about the character but if you have concerns too we could go in to Robert together and—

R J: I hate the fucking raccoon.

ANNE: Really.

R J: He never ran the concept by me. He just said we're doing it.

ANNE: Shit.

R J: I didn't get it. At all. So I had to try like twenty times 'til he found one he likes.

ANNE: He's settled on a drawing?

R J: Yeah, the one that sucks the worst.

ANNE: Oh god.

R J: It's rancid. It's cute. I don't want my name anywhere near it.

ANNE: If you can't make the character good I don't have a chance. Everything you do is—

(R J puts his hand on her breast.)

ANNE: Wow. *(She holds it there, leans in towards him to hide the hand, looks around.)* Too bad we don't have private offices like he does, huh. So, did you go to art school?

R J: Shh. Close your eyes. Imagine this.

(ANNE closes her eyes as R J massages her.)

R J: You have a friend who's in touch with Darcy. Darcy's always asking him how things are going here. She gets a sense Robert's struggling so she considers taking the show away from Robert, doing it in-house at the network with your friend taking the lead. He plans to bring Jill along, and you too. So it's the same creative team but suddenly everything's different. You don't have someone telling you to do stuff that sucks. You can do what comes naturally. What feels right and good, you know it's good and the others know it's good too, and you know they know because of what

they're doing with it, you love what they're doing with
what you're doing so you love doing it even more,
putting it out there, feeling it good, getting it right and
strong and good every day you can't wait to go in. *(He
stops massaging her.)* Okay?

ANNE: *(Opening her eyes)* Okay.

Scene 7. Holly and Doctor Jill

HOLLY: You really like Cumfy Mumfy better than
Bruno's World?

DR JILL: Bruno's too wild and crazy for kids.

HOLLY: He is really wild.

DR JILL: To do stuff that's titillating or clever for adults,
that kids can't even get, it can give them nightmares.

HOLLY: For sure. How do you feel about Robert's idea
for the overweight raccoon?

DR JILL: Well Holly, I'm disappointed. He'd said he
wanted to really do something bold with the show, I
had an idea for how to do that, and his response seems
like such a tiny step.

HOLLY: But you wouldn't complain outside the
company, right?

DR JILL: What do you mean?

HOLLY: Somebody's been complaining to Darcy about
the character.

DR JILL: You think I did?

HOLLY: Robert thinks maybe it was R J.

DR JILL: So you came to ask me about R J's private
conversations? Why would you do that?

HOLLY: Well, you and him, you know.

DR JILL: No, I don't know.

HOLLY: I guess, I just thought, since he did those drawings for you.

DR JILL: Robert changed the way the Duck walks for you, so don't go making assumptions.

HOLLY: I'm not making assumptions.

(DR JILL snaps her fingers and stomps her foot. HOLLY gasps.)

DR JILL: You should think about what you said to me.

HOLLY: I'm sorry.

DR JILL: I expected better from you.

(HOLLY cries.)

HOLLY: I didn't want to ask you this stuff, Robert made me. I totally respect you, I want to learn from you and work with you and help with your book, you're my total role model, but Robert's putting me in this position and now I got you all angry.

DR JILL: I'm not angry. Listen. Darcy's interested in R J's career, so she asks him how things are going and he tells her. That's all.

HOLLY: Okay. *(Sniffles)* Thanks.

Scene 8. Robert and R J

ROBERT: You're doing great work.

R J: Thanks.

ROBERT: You take my ideas and run with them really well.

R J: It's fun.

ROBERT: Oh good. So I was surprised to hear you complained about how things are going to Darcy.

R J: That was just about the raccoon.

ROBERT: So you did complain.

R J: About the raccoon.

ROBERT: What did you say?

R J: I said I didn't get what you were thinking.

ROBERT: You told her that.

R J: Yeah.

ROBERT: Why didn't you tell me?

R J: I did.

ROBERT: You didn't. You had questions. But you didn't say you had no idea what I was thinking. Why didn't you tell me before you complained to Darcy.

R J: There's no point.

ROBERT: No point?

R J: You always know what you want.

ROBERT: That's right I know what I want. The show came from me, my gut, so I can see what it needs, so you have to trust me, and if something bothers you, don't tell Darcy, tell me.

R J: But you just said you won't listen.

ROBERT: I said I will listen.

R J: "You have to trust me". You just said.

ROBERT: That's right.

R J: So if I see a problem—

ROBERT: You're a jerk. That's what you are. You're an arrogant little jerk. I spent years building this company, and you come along and try to mess things up. You think I wouldn't have a show without you? Is that what you think?

R J: Yeah.

ROBERT: You think without you I wouldn't have a show? You really think that? You think that?

R J: Yeah.

ROBERT: Let me hear you say it. Say it.

R J: I think—

ROBERT: Let me tell you, I would have a show. It would be exactly the same show.

R J: You wouldn't have the characters.

ROBERT: I'd have all the characters. They're all mine.

R J: I made them.

ROBERT: I created them. I named them. I gave them personalities. I described how they look. Without you they'd look a little different and that's all, and let me tell you something else, you think you've done so much, you haven't done crap, those other shows you've worked on are crap, I don't care what the ratings are, everybody knows they're crap. This is your first chance to do something really good, I'm giving you a chance so don't go shooting off your mouth. Okay?

(R J *shrugs.*)

ROBERT: What? You'll keep talking to Darcy?

(R J *shrugs.*)

ROBERT: I didn't want to use this. (*He takes out a duck puppet.*) Darcy gave us the duck puppets. I don't think she'd like to hear about the patch of worn-down fur inside yours.

R J: Who knows about this.

ROBERT: Just the person who discovered it.

R J: You know. So you discovered it.

ROBERT: Right.

R J: The worn-down part is way up in the back of the head, the only way you could have found it is if you were using the duck for the same thing I was.

ROBERT: Damn it.

R J: Do you go around the office at night checking them all out for softness?

(ROBERT *looks away.*)

R J: Are they all wool?

ROBERT: *(Refers to a smaller puppet)* This one's velvet.

R J: Nice.

ROBERT: Yeah.

(R J *and* ROBERT *stroke each other's ducks.*)

Scene 9. Doctor Jill and Anne

(They pretend to work on a script, speaking secretively to one another. CAPITALIZED WORDS are spoken loudly to throw observers off track.)

ANNE: Did R J back down?

DR JILL: He let Robert think he's backing down but he's not. And Darcy's close to making a move.

ANNE: REALLY GOOD NOTE.

DR JILL: OH THANKS.

ANNE: Wow.

DR JILL: How do you think R J would be as a boss.

ANNE: Better than Robert. Why.

DR JILL: R J decides things by impulse, what he feels in the moment. I wonder how we'd work with that.

ANNE: Right.

DR JILL: You and I can always talk things out.

ANNE: We disagree but—

DR JILL: We always—

ANNE: —talk things out, sure.

DR JILL: So. What if we tell Darcy we'll only stay on if R J shares control with us three ways.

ANNE: You and me would be a majority of the three.

DR JILL: Exactly.

ANNE: What would you want to do about the raccoon?

DR JILL: Lose it.

ANNE: Great.

DR JILL: As long as one character, at some point, is physically challenged.

ANNE: Make the call.

DR JILL: GOOD MEETING.

ANNE: GOOD MEETING.

(As DR JILL tries to hug ANNE, ANNE shoves her away.)

ANNE: Shit, shit, sorry.

DR JILL: We have trust issues.

ANNE: I'm so fucked up, please let me try again, we need to get through this.

DR JILL: All right, but slowly, okay?

(ANNE and DR JILL slowly go into a hug. When they make contact ANNE gasps.)

DR JILL: We did it. Okay. You can let go now.

ANNE: You're really tense, Jill.

DR JILL: Am I?

ANNE: Like a rock.

Scene 10. Robert and Holly

(ROBERT *sits frozen, hyperventilating.*)

HOLLY: So Darcy wants you to show everybody the rough cut of the pilot, get their feedback, get things out in the open, it doesn't mean she's taking the show away from you. They'll love what they see and they'll stop complaining to her.

ROBERT: They're going to hate the pilot. I redid everything they gave me.

HOLLY: Maybe if you just change the one character they don't like—

ROBERT: That would be like replacing my brother.

HOLLY: The rough cut'll be done Friday, so should I schedule a showing for then?

ROBERT: They'd love the pilot if I were dead.

HOLLY: She's holding back the budget til we do this.

(ROBERT's *entire body shakes.*)

ROBERT: Can I see your bare foot?

(HOLLY *shows* ROBERT *her foot. His shaking subsides.*)

ROBERT: Okay, Friday.

Scene 11. Holly and R J

(R J *draws.* HOLLY *walks past drinking juice from a small carton. They pretend not to see each other.*)

HOLLY: Jill and Anne. (*Makes hand gesture of gabbing mouth, while making 2-beat clucking sound with her tongue.*) To Darcy.

(R J *smacks a desk.*)

R J: This shakes things up. On Friday, after we speak truth to shit-head, if things go my way,

HOLLY: *(Whispers)* Oh god.

R J: They're out, you're in.

(HOLLY squeezes her juice, it squirts.)

Scene 12. All five characters. A cake, a knife.

ROBERT: How is everybody.

DR JILL: Good.

ANNE: Good.

R J: Okay.

ROBERT: Everything's going okay?

DR JILL: Sure.

R J: Mm hmm.

HOLLY: Did you want me to cut the cake?

ROBERT: Um, maybe after the show. Anyway, listen.
To say things about how things are going here, to
anybody on the outside, if you can't say them to me,
it's really bad form. So, does anybody have anything to
say? Now's your chance.

DR JILL: I suppose if I had one comment it would be
that sometimes suggestions aren't given quite as much
weight as they might be, so it feels like we might be
being humored instead of really being part of a team.

ROBERT: Huh. Anybody else?

ANNE: *(Mumbles softly)* I guess, yeah, the feeling,
sometimes, of being given changes, and feeling like,
yeah, like she said.

ROBERT: Hm. Any more?

R J: You don't listen.

ROBERT: No, I do. I do listen. Right? Anyone? What do
you think Holly?

HOLLY: I think it's an amazing show, and their comments are good because it can always be more amazing, anything can.

ROBERT: Oh. Okay. Well, we don't need to watch this if you people aren't in the mood.

DR JILL: Oh no, let's watch it.

R J: Let's see.

ANNE/HOLLY: Sure./Yeah.

ROBERT: Okay then.

(HOLLY *handles a remote control. They watch.*)

(*We hear, but don't see, the T V.*)

(*From the TV : "Hey Little Duck." "Hey Little Pig." "Wanna take a walk around the pond?" "Okey doke!" Sweet music plays.*)

(*As the sweet music continues:*)

(ROBERT *stands behind the other four, watches them watching.*)

(*He picks up the cake knife, brings it to his throat, then his heart. He turns the knife away from himself, towards* R J.)

(R J *turns, sees* ROBERT *pointing the knife at him, lunges at* ROBERT. *They fight.*)

(ANNE, DR JILL, *and* HOLLY *struggle to pull the men apart. The knife falls.*)

(HOLLY *pulls* ROBERT *away from* R J, *holds him back.*)

(ANNE *and* DR JILL *hold* R J, *kiss him.*)

(ANNE *pushes* DR JILL *away from* R J, DR JILL *pushes* ANNE, ANNE *and* DR JILL *struggle and begin making out.*)

(R J *watches* ANNE *and* DR JILL *make out, picks up a duck puppet and rubs it against his body.*)

(ROBERT *kisses* HOLLY. *She pushes him off and grabs onto* R J. *As* HOLLY *kisses* R J, ROBERT *pulls off her shoe and sucks her foot.*)

(R J *gets free of* HOLLY, *grabs* ROBERT *from behind and humps him.*)

(HOLLY *grabs onto* ANNE *and* DR JILL *who try to push her away.*)

(*From the T V: "Hey Little Duck."*)

(*All stop mauling each other and watch the screen, transfixed.*)

(*From the T V: "Hey Little Raccoon."*)

(*They give a small laugh, in perfect unison.*)

(*From the T V: "I [Hiccup]"*)

(*They give a bigger laugh.*)

(*From the T V: "I think you're great."*)

(*They sigh.*)

(*From the T V: "Wanna dance?" "Okey doke." Music swells.*)

(*They gasp, blown away.*)

(*As the music finishes, they sit in silence.*)

DR JILL: Robert, when you took my suggestion for a challenged character and changed it to the raccoon, you were so right. It really does feel exactly like I'd hoped and I'm so proud.

R J: It really does work in the context. It's like the coolest of all my characters.

ANNE: Oh thanks. Sometimes when you're at the computer a character just starts speaking, it's so amazing when that happens.

ROBERT: You've all done amazing work on my show.

HOLLY: I'm so happy with how Little Duck walks.

R J: Me too.

DR JILL: He's a tremendous character.

ANNE/HOLLY/ROBERT/R J: Thanks.

HOLLY: Robert. I was bad. I guess I started thinking, maybe this wasn't the place for me. So I talked to someone. I was totally wrong.

DR JILL: Me too.

ANNE: Yeah.

R J: Sorry about that.

ROBERT: It's okay.

R J: And sorry about just now, too.

DR JILL: That was inappropriate.

ANNE: Yeah.

HOLLY: We got carried away.

ROBERT: Big groups get so crazy. I'll try to keep meetings smaller.

R J: Definitely.

DR JILL: Yeah.

HOLLY: For sure.

(Pause)

ROBERT: I guess we can have cake now.

DR JILL/HOLLY: Sounds good./All right.

(Pause)

ANNE: How about a group hug?

ROBERT: Okey doke.

(They move together, slowly, embrace.)

END OF PLAY

IN THE MIDDLE OF THE NIGHT

IN THE MIDDLE OF THE NIGHT was originally produced in Marathon 2011 at Ensemble Studio Theatre (William Carden, Artistic Director; Paul Alexander Slee, Executive Director). The cast and creative contributors were:

DAN ....Jared McGuire
SHERRY ....Irene Longshore
ELISE ....Helen Coxe
JACK .... Scott Sowers

Director..Robert Davenport
Costumes... Erica Evans
Sound .... Benjamin Furiga
Lights ....Greg MacPherson
Set .... Jason Simms
Props .... Starlet Jacobs
Choreography... Wendy Seyb

CHARACTERS

DAN, *18*
SHERRY, *18*
ELISE, *40s*
JACK, *50s*

(DAN *and* SHERRY, *in a dark room with boxes*)

SHERRY: Take off your shirt.

(DAN *takes off his shirt.*)

SHERRY: Mess up your hair.

(DAN *messes up his hair.*)

SHERRY: Crouch down.

(DAN *crouches, like a cat ready to stalk.*)

SHERRY: Come and get me.

(DAN *starts towards* SHERRY, *slows to a stop.*)

SHERRY: What.

DAN: Nothing. (*He starts again, slows.*)

SHERRY: You don't want to be here.

DAN: It's just, forcing open a window, in the middle of the night, if a building's closed, I'm not used to that.

SHERRY: So I'm bad. Is that it? I'm a bad person.

DAN: No.

SHERRY: I'm not going to keep meeting on the soccer field, Danny, that's boring. Or on the roof of your dorm. Bore-ing-guh.

DAN: I'm not saying—

SHERRY: "Forcing open?" It was unlocked. Who are we disturbing here, the boxes?

DAN: I didn't say that.

SHERRY: Put your shirt on.

DAN: Sherry.

SHERRY: Put it on.

(DAN *puts his shirt on.*)

SHERRY: You don't like me.

DAN: What?

SHERRY: When your friends pass by you act like I don't exist. You don't look at me and you don't talk to me. Maybe we should stop seeing each other.

(DAN *covers his eyes, pants.*)

(SHERRY *waits.*)

DAN: I've never been in anything like this. You have to be patient with me. The other day, when I saw you out the window, I walked out of class to be with you, right?

SHERRY: I know. And I appreciate that.

DAN: When I'm with you and I see my friends I get weird. I don't know why. But the thing is, since we started up, everyone I used to hang out with, everything I used to do, it's all pointless and stupid. Bore-ing-guh. There's nothing but you that I can stand for ten seconds. So don't say…what you said.

SHERRY: I would never end it. You'll have to be the one.

DAN: I never will.

SHERRY: I've never been in anything like this either, you know.

DAN: You haven't?

SHERRY: (*Suddenly angry*) You don't believe me?

DAN: I—

SHERRY: You think I do this with everybody? How can you say that? Fuck you.

DAN: I didn't say that.

(DAN *hides his face, hunches over.*)

SHERRY: I'm sorry I said fuck you.

(DAN *nods, still hunched over.*)

SHERRY: You can do this, right?

DAN: *(Standing up straight, shouts)* I can do this thing.

SHERRY: Sometimes I say stuff. You know that.

DAN: I love you, Sherry.

SHERRY: I love you too.

DAN: I want to make you happy.

SHERRY: I'll never be happy.

DAN: Never?

SHERRY: When other people's bodies change the world starts to feel different, being inside their skin has a whole different feeling. But that can't happen for me. It's just how I'm made.

DAN: How can you—

SHERRY: Don't argue. Everyone has to accept what they are. And I'm not being song-lyric I mean it.

DAN: I wasn't saying you're being song-lyric.

SHERRY: Good. *(Beat)* So what should we do.

DAN: You wanted me to crouch like a cougar.

SHERRY: I don't feel like that now.

DAN: What do you feel like?

SHERRY: Why do I always have to be the one to choose?

DAN: You choose great stuff.

SHERRY: Don't you have ideas? Ever?

DAN: Yes.

SHERRY: So have an idea.

DAN: I want to do what you want to do.

SHERRY: Suggest something.

DAN: What should I—

SHERRY: *(Yells)* Anything.

DAN: Let's run.

SHERRY: No. Hey I know. Let's—

DAN: Oh wait. Can we do that thing where you jump onto my back?

SHERRY: Really?

DAN: Yeah.

SHERRY: When I did that it scared you.

DAN: I wasn't expecting it.

SHERRY: You got so mad.

DAN: I messed up. But now I'm ready. Try me again.

SHERRY: When the time is right. Right now, let's do our dance.

(Hardly looking at each other, hardly touching, DAN and SHERRY dance slowly, in perfect unison. The dance finishes.)

SHERRY: We're amazing. Now let's look for a fire escape.

DAN: Shirt off?

SHERRY: Yeah.

(DAN takes off his shirt.)

(Sounds outside the door)

SHERRY: Is that who I think?

DAN: Uh huh.

SHERRY: I shouldn't meet her?

DAN: No.

SHERRY: Get inside a box.

(DAN hides inside a box. SHERRY is hidden behind it.)

(ELISE *and* JACK *enter.*)

ELISE: When I say "that's him pull over" you pull over
the car, you don't drive around the block looking for
a parking place, and when I say he went in through
the window you don't go looking for a door and you
don't stand there explaining five ways I could hurt
myself, you hold the garbage can steady and you help
me climb up and then my god if you think there's an
elevator show me where it is already, it doesn't do any
good to say you think there's an elevator, "there must
be an elevator", "it says there's an elevator", what
good does that do? And now he could be anywhere
in the building, we're going to have to go through
thirty rooms on four floors while somehow making
sure he doesn't get back down the stairs and out of the
building. Are you happy?

JACK: You're sure he saw you?

ELISE: *(Mocking)* "You're sure he saw you?" I called his
name and he ran, yes I'm sure he saw me, why else
would he climb into an empty building in the middle
of the night?

JACK: Because he's a teenager, Elise.

ELISE: He's walking out in the middle of classes, his
advisor's worried, his teachers, his friends, why do you
argue?

JACK: When my kids were his age they got drunk, they
got tattoos—

ELISE: That has nothing to do with anything, do you
hear what I'm saying?, I feel like I'm talking to a—what
are you doing. Jack.

JACK: *(Taking out a cigarette)* What's it look like I'm
doing?

ELISE: This is a university, they have rules.

JACK: Like about climbing in the window?

ELISE: You're not smoking here.

JACK: For five hours in the car I didn't smoke.

ELISE: I said—

JACK: I'll go outside.

(ELISE *follows as* JACK *starts off.*)

ELISE: No. No. What you're going to do is, you're going to wait on the stairs, and I'm going to go from room to room—

(*A sound from the box.* ELISE *hurries back in with* JACK, *gestures that* JACK *should lift up the box, which he does, to reveal* DAN *sitting there.*)

(*Though* SHERRY *is now in plain view:* SHERRY *is invisible to* JACK *and* ELISE. *Only* DAN *can see or hear her, and she speaks only to* DAN.)

ELISE: (*To* DAN) Hi honey.

SHERRY: (*To* DAN) Are you going to ignore me with her like you do with your friends?

ELISE: You remember Jack.

JACK: Hey Dan.

ELISE: We had a free weekend so we thought we'd stay at the inn, maybe drop by your dorm in the morning, but we saw you out and about so…

SHERRY: Look at me. You can look at me at least. Why can't you look at me?

ELISE: Hello? Anybody there?

SHERRY: You're hurting me. You know that, right? I'm in pain. You know that I'm in pain.

DAN: (*To* SHERRY) I'm sorry.

ELISE: You're sorry what.

SHERRY: That was a big step. Thank you.

JACK: We're over here, Dan.

ELISE: Why is your shirt off, honey? Why is your hair like that?

SHERRY: Don't answer her.

ELISE: What are you doing up here by yourself in the middle of the night?

SHERRY: Shh shh.

ELISE: *(To* JACK*)* Is he on drugs?, it's like he's hallucinating. *(To* DAN*)* Are you on drugs, Danny?

SHERRY: Okay. One word.

DAN: *(To* ELISE*)* No.

ELISE: It's not drugs, I know that. Are you feeling a lot of pressure, with the courses?

SHERRY: Answer.

DAN: *(To* ELISE*)* I

SHERRY: One word.

ELISE: These aren't hard questions to answer.

SHERRY: She's like you said.

*(*DAN *nods to* SHERRY *and laughs.)*

ELISE: Danny. Look at me. Is this a game?

SHERRY: She's being totally what.

DAN: She's being song-lyric, yeah. *(Laughs)*

ELISE: *(To* JACK*)* My uncle was this way, they put him in a home, he never got better.

JACK: Elise.

ELISE: I wanted to come up the minute he stopped taking my calls but you said teenagers do that.

SHERRY: It's getting hot in here, right? Let's get some air. Now. Go.

(DAN *dashes towards the door. Jack catches him and holds him.)*

ELISE: What are you doing put him down.

JACK: You want him to get away?

ELISE: You're hurting him.

JACK: I'm not hurting him.

ELISE: Let him go, stand by the door, let him go, block the door.

(JACK *lets* DAN *go,* DAN *runs in circles,* SHERRY *cheers him on.)*

SHERRY: Oh my god oh god she can't stop us now because we're totally defining our own path whatever path we want it's ours you're so special to me I could drink a case of you right now we're totally free everything we do from here on in is our own definition.

(DAN *crouches and crawls to* SHERRY, *she pulls up her shirt.)*

(ELISE *turns away, tries to hide her sobs, makes a muffled choking sound.* DAN *slows down.)*

SHERRY: Ignore that sound. You don't hear it.

DAN: *(To* ELISE*)* Why are you sad?

ELISE: Because I don't understand how you're acting.

(DAN *puts on his shirt.)*

SHERRY: Oh Danny. This isn't easy.

(DAN *straightens his hair.)*

SHERRY: You look ridiculous.

ELISE: So Dan…

SHERRY: Here it comes.

ELISE: I thought maybe you'd come home for a while...

SHERRY: She wins. I get it.

ELISE: ...See if we can find someone who can talk to you and maybe help you feel more comfortable. Your bedroom's just like you left it.

SHERRY: Go. Go.

(DAN *walks away from* SHERRY.)

SHERRY: I found you in the courtyard. I found you under your desk. I found you in the middle of an empty field in the total darkness. I'll always find you.

DAN: *(To* SHERRY*)* I don't want you to find me. I want you to come with me.

(SHERRY *charges* DAN *and leaps onto his back. Then she slides down from his back, and* DAN *and* SHERRY *do their dance.)*

(ELISE *watches, pants loudly.)*

JACK: *(To* ELISE*)* He's not your uncle. Okay? Whatever this is, we'll figure it out, one step at a time, and we'll deal with it. There are medicines, whatever it takes, he'll get through this. And you'll get through it, okay? Maybe things won't go the way you expected for him. Maybe they'll go a different way. But he's still your kid. And you're still going to love him.

(ELISE *holds onto* JACK.)

(*As* DAN *and* SHERRY *continue to dance they speak softly to one another.)*

SHERRY: Will we be together more and more? Or less and less?

DAN: I don't know.

SHERRY: Will you wear you hair like she wants or the way I like it?

DAN: I don't know.

SHERRY: Will anyone ever accept me as part of your life?

DAN: I don't know.

SHERRY: What do you know?

DAN: You.

(As SHERRY *clings to* DAN, DAN *offers a hand to* ELISE. ELISE *holds onto* JACK's *arm with one hand, holds* DAN's *hand with the other. All four are linked.)*

JACK: We'll go by his place, pick up his stuff.

ELISE: Sure.

JACK: Then we'll pass by the inn and cancel the room.

ELISE: Okay.

DAN: I can do this thing.

SHERRY: We're amazing.

(The four start off. As SHERRY *hangs onto* DAN *he has to drag her, so* ELISE *leads him along while being supported by* JACK. *But they get into an odd rhythm, a sort of strange dance, and move on together.)*

END OF PLAY

NIGHT RULES

NIGHT RULES premiered in Marathon 2001 at Ensemble Studio Theatre (Curt Dempster, Artistic Director). The cast and creative contributors were:

ROB .... Thomas Lyons
BECKY .... Katherine Leask
KEN .... Joe Urla
ANDREA .... Geneva Carr

Director .... Jamie Richards
Lights .... Greg MacPherson
Set .... Charles Kirby
Costumes .... Jacqueline Firkins
Sound .... Robert Gould
Props .... Michelle McKiernan, Alison Weiss

CHARACTERS

ROB
BECKY
KEN
ANDREA

(ANDREA *and* KEN *sit with their guests* BECKY *and* ROB.)

BECKY: But he tortures her.

ANDREA: Of course he does.

ROB: He turns her room upside down.

BECKY: The minute we're not looking.

ANDREA: Of course he tortures her.

KEN: Because you let her sleep with you.

ANDREA: He'll stop torturing her the minute you stop letting her get into bed with you.

BECKY: But she wakes up screaming.

ROB: In the middle of the night.

BECKY: She has these nightmares.

ANDREA: I have nightmares, don't you have nightmares?

KEN: You can't let her get into bed with you.

BECKY: So we should just let her scream?

ANDREA: Ours used to scream.

KEN: They both used to.

ROB: And you just let them, right?

ANDREA: If you let them get into bed with you—

KEN: It rewards them.

ANDREA: It teaches them to scream.

KEN: You're training them.

ANDREA: You're instilling this need in them.

KEN: Who is it helping.

ROB: *(To* BECKY*)* Didn't I say that, honey?

ANDREA: Your bed is yours.

KEN: They've got to understand that.

BECKY: You really just let them scream for as long as…

ANDREA: It'll be hard the first night.

KEN: Give it three nights.

ROB: We did try telling her she couldn't sleep with us.

BECKY: But I kept giving in.

ANDREA: You can't do that.

KEN: Saying she can't sleep with you and then letting her sleep with you is the worst possible thing.

ROB: *(To* BECKY*)* Remember I said that?

ANDREA: That teaches them you don't mean what you say.

KEN: You're training them to defy you.

ROB: That's right.

ANDREA: Your words lose all meaning.

KEN: "Blah blah blah blah," that's all they hear after a while.

ANDREA: They need you to mean what you say.

KEN: It's very disturbing to a kid.

ANDREA: They're counting on you for consistency.

BECKY: You're right, I know.

ROB: *(To* BECKY*)* So if we say she can't sleep with us you can't let her sleep with us—

ANDREA: You really can't.

ROB: —or give her a jelly donut either.

KEN: You give your kids donuts?

BECKY: Jelly donuts have fruit.

KEN: Donuts are candy.

ROB: They're okay for breakfast but—

ANDREA: Maybe for a special treat.

KEN: They're fried sugar.

ANDREA: *(To* KEN*)* You buy them cereal that's saturated with sugar.

KEN: But it isn't also soaked in grease.

ROB: —we can't reward her with a jelly donut for screaming her head off.

ANDREA: When she wakes up in the middle of the night you can not reward her.

KEN: For her sake.

BECKY: I know you're right...

ANDREA: You can do this, believe me.

KEN: The thing is to be clear with her.

ANDREA: Agree on just how you're going to present the new rule.

KEN: Tell her together.

ANDREA: There can't be any division between the two of you.

KEN: Kids can sense division.

ROB: Okay, honey?

ANDREA: The least degree.

KEN: They run wild.

ANDREA: They need you two to be totally together.

KEN: Then you say, you know, "This is how it's going to be."

ANDREA: She wants mommy and daddy to be happy.

KEN: It's for her sake too.

BECKY: And if she comes into our bed—

ANDREA: No.

BECKY: But if she does get up and—

ANDREA: She doesn't.

ROB: Right.

ANDREA: She does not get into your bed. Period.

KEN: That's right.

BECKY: But if she—

ANDREA: She does not get into your bed.

KEN: Make that clear.

BECKY: How do we—

ANDREA: Allowance.

KEN: Something.

ANDREA: Decide your deterrents beforehand.

KEN: You don't want to be figuring that out in the middle of the night.

ANDREA: No desserts.

KEN: T V.

ANDREA: Something.

BECKY: But no matter how loud she screams—

KEN: she stays in bed.

ANDREA: She will stay there.

KEN: You can get up with her.

ANDREA: You can sing to her.

ROB: Hold her hand?

KEN: You can hold her hand.

ANDREA: But she stays in her bed.

KEN: And the screaming will stop.

ANDREA: It will stop.

KEN: She will sleep.

ROB: And we'll sleep.

ANDREA: You'll all sleep and you'll all be very glad.

KEN: That's right.

BECKY: I know.

(From upstairs, a child's voice: "Maaaaaaaahhhhhh meeeeeeeeeee." BECKY *stands.)*

ROB: We told the kids to let the grown-ups talk.

BECKY: She has let us talk.

ROB: For five minutes.

BECKY: I told her if she played with the kids I'd drop in.

ROB: But she hasn't played with the kids.

ANDREA: If you go up there now she'll take that as a sign.

KEN: You define "playing with the kids" by how long you wait before going up.

ANDREA: You're depriving her of the chance to find a way to play with the kids.

ROB: It's been five minutes.

BECKY: I told her...

KEN: *(To* ANDREA*)* If she told her she'd go up she should go up.

ANDREA: *(To* KEN*)* You're not helping her by saying that.

ROB: *(To* BECKY*)* If you go up when she calls after five minutes what does that say to the other kids?

ANDREA: *(To* ROB*)* What does it say to her brother is the question.

KEN: *(To* ANDREA*)* As hostess you shouldn't interfere with the agreement she made with her kid.

ANDREA: *(To* KEN*)* If a guest is about to fall down it's your responsibility to catch them.

ROB: *(To* BECKY*)* It's our Saturday night, honey.

KEN: *(To* ANDREA*)* If you make her uncomfortable about checking up on her kid she won't want to come again.

ANDREA: *(To* KEN*)* She won't want to come again if her kid is going to boss her around.

ROB: We were with the kids all day. We'll be with them all day tomorrow. It's Saturday night.

ANDREA: We never see you guys.

ROB: *(To* BECKY*)* You're always saying we never have time with grown-ups.

BECKY: Fine, I won't go up.

ANDREA: This allows the kids to have fun together.

ROB: *(To* BECKY*)* Don't not-go-up to punish me, honey.

BECKY: *(To* ROB*)* I'm not punishing you.

KEN: *(To* BECKY*)* If you really want to go up you shouldn't not-go-up to appease us.

BECKY: *(To* KEN*)* If everybody doesn't want me to go up I really don't want to go up.

(Seized by a sudden burst of passion ANDREA *and* ROB *start making out, unnoticed by* BECKY *and* KEN*.)*

KEN: *(To* BECKY*)* If you just do what you need to and be clear that's what you're doing everyone else will be fine.

BECKY: *(To* KEN*)* I guess I should go up and let her know that this is the last time.

KEN: *(To* BECKY*)* If that's what you need to do, then just do it.

*(*BECKY *and* KEN *notice* ANDREA *and* ROB. ANDREA *and* ROB *stop making out.)*

ROB: *(To* BECKY*)* It just happened.

ANDREA: *(To* KEN*)* I needed something that I didn't know I need.

ROB: *(To* BECKY*)* I was watching myself...just do things.

BECKY: *(To* ROB*)* You can't be with me any more.

ROB: *(To* BECKY*)* Honey.

KEN: *(To* ANDREA*)* You have to cut it out completely or I won't stay with you.

ANDREA: *(To* KEN*)* I can't just cut it out because I need something.

KEN: *(To* ANDREA*)* Then I'm leaving you.

ANDREA: *(To* KEN*)* Don't. Please.

KEN: *(To* ANDREA*)* I have to.

ROB: *(To* ANDREA*)* Since I can't be with her, if he's not with you, can I stay with you?

ANDREA: *(To* ROB*)* If he's not with me...yes you can stay with me.

KEN: *(To* BECKY*)* Can I stay with you?

BECKY: Even if I let you...stay with me...you can't get into bed with me. No one can get into bed with me.

KEN: I don't want to stay with someone if I can't get into bed with her. I'd rather get my own place.

ANDREA: *(To* KEN*)* The kids should stay with me.

KEN: *(To* ANDREA*)* They're my kids too.

ANDREA: *(To* KEN*)* You can have them on weekends but I get them on holidays.

KEN: *(To* ANDREA*)* A father should be able to see more of his children than that.

ANDREA: *(To* KEN*)* Actually you should take them one week night too because I'll need a night off.

KEN: *(To* ANDREA*)* Week nights are hard for me.

ANDREA: *(To* KEN*)* I think you can be responsible for your children one night a week.

KEN: *(To* ANDREA*)* I'm taking them Friday night, all day Saturday, Saturday night, and all day Sunday. You can take your children four week nights.

BECKY: *(To* ROB*)* My children are staying with me.

ROB: *(To* BECKY*)* You have to share them.

BECKY: *(To* ROB*)* No one can take my children away from their mother. Except weekends. And the month of August.

ROB: *(To* BECKY*)* They're my kids too. I'm not sure about August.

KEN: I'll take all the kids in August if someone else will take July.

ANDREA: If she takes them the week of the Fourth we'll take them the rest of July.

ROB: *(To* ANDREA*)* All four kids at once for three weeks, honey?

KEN: Whoever they're with, they can't stay up til all hours.

ANDREA: That's right, the rules have to be the same whoever they're with or they'll go nuts.

KEN: We'll all go nuts.

ANDREA: One set of rules for all the kids. Whoever they're with.

KEN: We have to.

ANDREA: We'll need to agree on bedtimes.

ROB: Bedtimes and showers. And T V watching.

ANDREA: And what they should call us.

KEN: They'll all call me Fred.

ANDREA: Fred?

KEN: Their kids. Our kids. Everyone will call me Fred. From now on I'm Fred everyone. You have to call me Fred. I'm Fred.

ANDREA: Plus we all need to agree that whether the kids are with us, or her, or Fred, when they wake up screaming—

KEN: That's right they're bound to wake up screaming.

ANDREA: Of course they'll wake up screaming.

KEN: This will be a tough time for them.

ANDREA: We'll have to let them come into bed with us.

ROB: *(To* ANDREA*)* You're sure, honey?

ANDREA: For a while.

KEN: During a time like this you have to.

ANDREA: To let them know with all the change you're still there for them.

KEN: Then back to the old rules gradually.

ROB: Right.

ANDREA: That's right.

BECKY: No. I'm not sharing my bed with anyone.

ROB: *(To* BECKY*)* Just for the first month, *(To* ANDREA*)* right honey?

BECKY: No one sleeps with me. Period.

ANDREA: But if we let them into our bed when they're with us and she doesn't let them in her bed when they're with her—

ROB: *(To* BECKY*)* You're not going to give them jelly donuts, are you?

KEN: We can agree no donuts, right?

ROB: Except for breakfast.

KEN: My kids can't have candy for breakfast.

ANDREA: Donuts have a lot more flour than candy.

KEN: And a lot more grease.

ROB: *(To* BECKY*)* We won't give them donuts for breakfast if you don't give them donuts in the middle of the night.

ANDREA: We could all give them donuts for dessert and call it cake.

BECKY: I'll give them jelly donuts when they're screaming, and when they're crying, and when they're fighting, then I'll cut the supply down, way down, but they'll keep hoping, for this memory, it'll just be a memory, they'll lie there in the dark dreaming of the powder on their lips and their throats and they'll wake up shivering and screaming their heads off because there won't be any jelly donuts ever on the face of the earth.

(A voice from upstairs calls: "Mmaaaaaaaaahhhhh meeeeeeeeee." BECKY *sits calmly.* ANDREA *and* ROB *cling to one another.* KEN *hugs himself and rocks. "Mmmaaaaaaahhhhhh meeeeeeee. Mmaaaaaaaaaaaaaahhhh meeeeeeeeeeee…")*

END OF PLAY

LIGHT YEARS

Stage production rights licensed by Playscripts Inc.

The one-act version of LIGHT YEARS, sometimes referred to as LIGHT YEARS, PART ONE: FRESHMAN YEAR, premiered in Marathon 2000 at Ensemble Studio Theatre (Curt Dempster, Artistic Director). The cast and creative contributors were:

COURTNEY .... Anne Marie Nest
DAPHNE .... Sarah Rose
DOUG .... Paul Batholomew
MICHAEL .... Ian Reed Kesler

Director .... Jamie Richards
Lights .... Greg MacPherson
Set .... Warren Karp
Costumes .... Amela Baksic
Sound .... Beatrice Terry
Props .... Cynthia Franks

CHARACTERS

COURTNEY
DAPHNE
DOUG
MICHAEL

*(Living room of a freshman double. Door to bedroom. Door
to hall. Desk with chair. Closet. Couch. Crate)*

*(*COURTNEY *and* DAPHNE*)*

DAPHNE: So if I wear these sunglasses—

COURTNEY: Philosophy.

DAPHNE: They'll see me as—

COURTNEY: Lit major, comp lit, philosophy, psych.

DAPHNE: But if I go with this pair—

COURTNEY: Engineer.

DAPHNE: Engineer.

COURTNEY: Exactly.

DAPHNE: So I have…

COURTNEY: The choice.

DAPHNE: Right.

COURTNEY: Deep or diligent.

*(*DAPHNE *thinks.)*

COURTNEY: Or you could go to the picnic open, like
me. Open to sunshine. Open to the breeze. Open to law
school.

DAPHNE: Right.

COURTNEY: Any choice has its pluses. I'm just saying
that before you get pegged, you should decide.

DAPHNE: Right.

COURTNEY: Same goes for the photo.

DAPHNE: The photo.

COURTNEY: On your desk.

DAPHNE: Oh yeah.

COURTNEY: That photo says, to those dropping by on their way to the picnic, that you have someone, and that you're taken.

DAPHNE: Right.

COURTNEY: I have lots of someones. But I'm not taken.

DAPHNE: Right.

COURTNEY: I have friends who are taken, but want to appear untaken. That's their business.

DAPHNE: Right.

COURTNEY: I even have a friend who has no one, but wants to appear taken, for strategic purposes.

DAPHNE: Right.

COURTNEY: So anything goes. It's all up to you.

(DAPHNE nods.)

COURTNEY: So? Do you want to appear taken?

(DAPHNE thinks.)

COURTNEY: Let's work backwards. Do you have someone?

(DAPHNE thinks.)

COURTNEY: Have you ever had someone?

DAPHNE: This guy, we'd talk about everything, one time it was raining and there were all these sounds, the noises were us, saying and doing those things, that people say and do.

COURTNEY: So you have had someone.

DAPHNE: I can't remember.

COURTNEY: But you do want to have someone.

DAPHNE: Yes. Yes.

COURTNEY: So you'll put away the photo.

DAPHNE: Right.

COURTNEY: And the cross.

DAPHNE: The...

COURTNEY: Around your neck.

DAPHNE: This is a cross?

COURTNEY: It looks like a cross.

DAPHNE: Right.

COURTNEY: I'm not saying bury it, I'm just saying be aware.

DAPHNE: Aware.

COURTNEY: Of the whole question.

DAPHNE: Uh huh...

COURTNEY: Born again. Or the other extreme. Free spirit.

DAPHNE: Right.

COURTNEY: We're talking about your most fundamental values.

DAPHNE: My most fundamental values.

COURTNEY: Exactly.

DAPHNE: Which are...

COURTNEY: Pursuit of truth. Love of humanity. I don't know.

DAPHNE: Right.

COURTNEY: Before heading to the picnic you need to ask yourself: is that symbol rooted in the exact message you want to send out?

DAPHNE: Right.

COURTNEY: So?

DAPHNE: I'll come up with the answers as we shop for a plant.

COURTNEY: Shop for a plant? Now?

(DAPHNE *sits frozen.*)

COURTNEY: Are you telling me…you want to skip the freshmen picnic?

(DAPHNE *sits frozen.*)

COURTNEY: Daphne. Outside that window, in a matter of minutes, our generation will assemble. For this chance to win a prime spot in their ranks you've spent your last three summers serving burgers, committed your Fridays to filing periodicals, and taken out loans you'll be repaying 'til you're disabled or forty or dead. So seize the moment. Select the impression that will leap from your front and ricochet through the crowd 'til you're burned in their brains as a—

DAPHNE: Philosophical lit major who's not religious and not taken.

COURTNEY: Good. So then…

DAPHNE: I can't put away the photo. Because I can't stand up. My legs, something funny.

COURTNEY: Listen to me. Daphne. You'll be fine, because you're blessed with something that will get you through no matter what the world throws at you: You're pure.

DAPHNE: Pure what.

COURTNEY: Inside you, is a basic goodness and honesty that's special.

DAPHNE: You see this after knowing me for two hours?

COURTNEY: I saw this after knowing you for two seconds. The things I'm encouraging you to consider are icing on the cake. That's all. We just want the right icing, for so very fine a cake.

DAPHNE: *(Sitting up)* This is all so easy for you.

COURTNEY: You think I'm the type who just, everything's easy?

DAPHNE: I didn't mean anything bad.

COURTNEY: I know you didn't. It's only that some people have tended to label me. You know. As the type. Gliding along. Not really meaning things. But the thing is, growing up, my mother couldn't be with us so I, always had to be the one smiling, but it isn't easy always being the one smiling, people don't realize that, but I need you to know that when I say things to you I really mean those things from my heart.

DAPHNE: I know that.

COURTNEY: Anyway. Before I open the door to let in potential escorts, let's both take a second.

(COURTNEY and DAPHNE sit. A "Special Song" plays from above. Instantly, both go into a trance.)

COURTNEY: Somebody upstairs has good taste in songs.

(COURTNEY and DAPHNE listen.)

DAPHNE: Sleeping late on a snow day.

COURTNEY: Driving home from the prom.

(When the song fades, they emerge from their trances. COURTNEY opens the door—to find DOUG standing there.)

(DOUG raises his voice at the end of many declarative sentences so they sound like questions.)

DOUG: The sunshine splashing across the banners? The flowers all over the place?, and everywhere you look the greatest people? Strumming guitars? Dancing around? Hugging? Every few steps a different song? Everyone so giving, so open? Can I come in?,

great room, so near the main entrance?, so near the
bathroom?, great view? *(Out window)* Hey Mom, go
home? *(To them)* So we're classmates, first-entry-mates?
So…do I hug you? Shake your hands? Kiss your
hands? Let me move your crate. *(He moves the crate.)*

COURTNEY/DAPHNE: Thank you./Thanks.

DOUG: Let me center your couch. *(He moves the couch,
grabs his back.)* The backache'll be no problem since I'm
already taking aspirin for a pulled thigh. What terrific
hair you have, and eyes. The atmosphere of giving and
kindness here is contagious?

COURTNEY: Iced tea?

DOUG: Everybody's trying new things? Reaching out?
Why iced tea.

COURTNEY: You moved our couch.

DOUG: I've never had iced tea. Why have I never had
iced tea. Because, maybe somewhere along the line I
was prejudiced? Smelled a skunk out the window and
thought: iced tea? So I wrote off iced tea and lived in
fear? But now it's time to leave the past behind and
have iced tea? *(Out window)* I'm fine Mom. *(To them)*
The other thing I love here is that no one talks about
grades or scores?, they talk about ideas? I wonder
if even though on the outside there are so many
differences between us, deep down we aren't really all
the same?

COURTNEY: Sugar?

DOUG: Sweetheart? Darling? And if even though the
individual conforms to society it isn't really society
that conforms to the individual in the end? Actually I'll
take it plain, here goes? *(He drinks, grabs a napkin, spits.)*
Better head upstairs for another aspirin? *(Starts out,
stops)* Any time you need a refrigerator moved just give

a knock? *(Starts out, stops)* Will you guys be going to the freshmen picnic?

COURTNEY: Surely.

DOUG: Can I juh-juh-juh-...juh-juh-juh-...juh-juh-juh- *(Grabs his tongue)* join you?

COURTNEY: Please do.

(DOUG goes into the closet. He comes back out.)

DOUG: Closet. *(He goes out the door.)*

COURTNEY: Nice.

DAPHNE: Nice.

COURTNEY: You find him nice?

DAPHNE: You think he's nice, right?

COURTNEY: He moved the crates. He moved the couch. There's no debating it: He's nice.

DAPHNE: Moving the couch hurt his back.

COURTNEY: But he acknowledged it up front.

DAPHNE: Right.

COURTNEY: He can talk about his pain.

DAPHNE: Sensitive.

COURTNEY: Exactly.

DAPHNE: Like Mark and Dave.

COURTNEY: Mark and

DAPHNE: Dave, from my school.

COURTNEY: Did you like Mark and Dave?

DAPHNE: I should have. They were so sensitive.

COURTNEY: With someone this sensitive you could discuss your philosophy.

DAPHNE: Right.

COURTNEY: But if you have concerns about shifting to comp lit or psych, he could discuss your fears.

DAPHNE: Right.

COURTNEY: Or your feelings about your faith…

DAPHNE: Do I have a faith?

COURTNEY: With him you could find out.

DAPHNE: Any issue.

COURTNEY: But he doesn't just talk.

DAPHNE: Right.

COURTNEY: He identifies a problem, then takes action.

DAPHNE: Aspirin.

COURTNEY: Takes aspirin, takes action, exactly. Which takes courage.

DAPHNE: Right.

COURTNEY: You should go to the picnic together.

DAPHNE: Just the two of us?

COURTNEY: He loved your eyes.

DAPHNE: Both of them.

COURTNEY: I noticed.

DAPHNE: Think he might be…musical?

COURTNEY: Were Mark and Dave musical?

DAPHNE: Dave played piano.

COURTNEY: This guy might well play piano.

DAPHNE: Jazz?

COURTNEY: I can see him enjoying jazz. Tapping, swaying.

DAPHNE: Can you see us together?

COURTNEY: On the dance floor. Leaning together. Strolling to the punch bowl. A single cup, passed back and forth. He shouts in your ear. You shout in his ear. He grins, you gulp, you dance.

DAPHNE: He enjoys dancing?

COURTNEY: Surely.

DAPHNE: *(Ecstatic)* At last. *(Suddenly furious)* God.

COURTNEY: What.

DAPHNE: Why did I let my parents buy me a ticket to fly home over midterm break when I could have had them fly out here.

COURTNEY: To meet Aspirin?

DAPHNE: For once I get a guy who shares dad's love for jazz and I can't bring them together til Labor Day when we'd rather be celebrating the end of our first summer living off-campus together with a weekend at the shore.

COURTNEY: Fly home for the Fourth.

DAPHNE: Aspirin'll be seeing his mom.

COURTNEY: If he rearranged crates for you he'll rearrange his schedule for you.

DAPHNE: *(Embracing* COURTNEY*)* I'm finally taking off.

(MICHAEL *enters with course cards.)*

MICHAEL: Eight credits from each of groups one and four excluding a writing course other than those in groups two or three unless granted permission by professor, advisor, counsellor, or dean. I could fill these out in time for the deadline but I'd rather insert that crate in my nostril. All day I've been feeling so much like a cartoon character that I have to keep pulling my skin to see if it stretches. *(He pulls his lips.)* Human. Hooray. *(He sits.)* So what if this *is* your fifth choice school, right? You've already survived fifth choice parents on a last choice planet. So where are you from?

How was your summer? Are you taking blah 101 so you can major in blah, or are you really pre-blah? Will you sign up for blah and go out for the blah or audition for blah? Oh if you went to blah well then you must know blah who I met backpacking through blah on blah.

COURTNEY: Iced tea?

MICHAEL: Why the fuck not.

(COURTNEY *hands* MICHAEL *iced tea. He drinks it all. He looks at them, they look at him.*)

MICHAEL: You guys going to the freshman blah blah?

COURTNEY: Surely.

MICHAEL: If I finish my blah should I blah?

COURTNEY: Please do.

(MICHAEL *goes.*)

DAPHNE: But how will I pull it off.

COURTNEY: It being…

DAPHNE: Dump Aspirin for Course Cards.

COURTNEY: Are you sure that's the move you want to make, at this point in time?

DAPHNE: Jazz with my parents? What was I thinking. That's what I came here to crawl out from under. Aspirin was about to drag me backwards. Til Course Cards snapped his lips and cracked my shell. Allowed me to stop pushing. To let down my smile and accept the quiet. I live to be quiet. I shine when I'm quiet. Did you hear how quiet I was?

COURTNEY: You were quiet.

DAPHNE: I don't want to crush Aspirin. But I can't let him drag me back to my days of Mark and Dave.

COURTNEY: I'll go to the picnic with Aspirin, leaving you free to invite Course Cards.

DAPHNE: Invite…

COURTNEY: March up there, mention you're going, ask him along.

DAPHNE: You really see us together?

COURTNEY: Midnight, late-autumn, two figures, out from the library, across the leaves in slow motion, a few syllables, a few nods, then silence, then a muffin, from his hand, to your lips, to his lips, to his room.

DAPHNE: Raisin?

COURTNEY: What else.

DAPHNE: You don't think he'll mind my cats.

COURTNEY: You have cats?

DAPHNE: I hope to. Someday.

COURTNEY: They'll curl up on his lap as he watches his cartoons.

DAPHNE: *(Embracing* COURTNEY*)* I'm finally moving on.

COURTNEY: But before heading up, I'd change out of school colors.

DAPHNE: School colors.

COURTNEY: On your top.

DAPHNE: These aren't school colors.

COURTNEY: Close enough.

*(*DAPHNE *gasps.)*

COURTNEY: For your tryst with Course Cards, you'll want to steer clear of school colors.

DAPHNE: He caught me in school colors.

COURTNEY: We'll erase the mis-impression from his mind…as I dig deep into my trunk, and cloak you in black.

DAPHNE: Black. *(Thinks)* You saved my life.

(COURTNEY goes into the bedroom.)

(DAPHNE takes out a phone, makes a call.)

DAPHNE: Pick up. I'm here. It's great. I won't be home for break. Call me. I won't be home this summer, I'm free, I'm flying, I can see…everything, all your crap, what *was* that. Call me I'll explain. You won't get it, how could you. You're so old. I've gone a million miles, you're staying still. You'll never get it. You'll never reach me. Call me.

(DAPHNE hangs up, moves around.)

(DOUG enters.)

DOUG: Everybody's starting to mingle in these little clusters?, The chicken smells great?

DAPHNE: I'm not going.

DOUG: Thank you for having the courage to stand up, to something so obligatory, so unnecessary, so how was your summer?

DAPHNE: I'll drop in on the picnic later.

DOUG: You're right, let the others break the ice? Your roommate already went but who cares, you're the one with the eyes, beautiful eyes? Did you like high school?

DAPHNE: Did I…

DOUG: A haze? Mine too?

DAPHNE: I need some time…

DOUG: So do I, before we go?

DAPHNE: Please let me finish my sentence.

DOUG: We're finishing each other's sentences? What does that say?

DAPHNE: Nothing.

DOUG: You're right, but as nothing was being said, what really happened?

DAPHNE: Time passed.

DOUG: Time passed, you're right, so I guess we should go?

DAPHNE: I have plans. But my roommate will go to the picnic with you when she's ready.

DOUG: Just me and her? Her hair lights up a room. It would be wonderful if she would hurry because my roommate's coming down and he has this tendency to whine that the earth is his last choice planet?

DAPHNE: That's your roommate?

DOUG: I like him and I think he's great but he's always breathing on people and tagging along?, I tried to slip out while he was doing his course cards but when he heard my plans he said he'd be right down?

(DAPHNE *hurries into the bedroom.*)

DAPHNE: Course Cards'll be right down.

COURTNEY: Here's your outfit.

(DOUG *follows* DAPHNE *into the bedroom.*)

DAPHNE: I need to change.

DOUG: Who reads Joyce? I love Joyce. Who collects stuffed animals?

(DAPHNE *hurries out from the bedroom into the living room, closing the bedroom door behind her.*)

DOUG: *(Behind door)* Who closed the door?

(DAPHNE *starts frantically changing her clothes.*)

DOUG: *(Behind door, to* COURTNEY*)* I'll wait out there til you're ready?

*(*DOUG *hurries out of the bedroom, closing the bedroom door behind him, sees* DAPHNE *undressed, stands frozen.)*

DOUG: I don't have any sisters but my cousins are girls?

*(*DAPHNE *goes into the living room closet, closes the door.)*

*(*DOUG *paces.)*

DAPHNE: *(From closet)* You've got me in short sleeves.

COURTNEY: *(From room)* It's still summer.

DAPHNE: *(From closet)* I hate my arms.

COURTNEY: *(From room)* Your arms are great.

DOUG: My birthday's September fifteenth? My favorite flavor's vanilla?

(There's a knock on the main door.)

DOUG: *(To himself)* Here he is to tag along on my date. *(He charges to the bedroom door, knocks.)*

COURTNEY & DAPHNE: *(From bedroom and closet)* Come in.

*(*DOUG *slips into the bedroom, closing the door behind him.)*

*(*MICHAEL *enters the living room, closing the door behind him.)*

*(*DAPHNE *steps out of the closet dressed in black.)*

DAPHNE: Fifth choice parents on a last choice planet. I love what you said. I'd been, wrestling with, something, and the minute you said it I thought, that's it.

*(*MICHAEL *doesn't respond.)*

DAPHNE: We don't choose our parents. We don't choose our planet.

(MICHAEL *doesn't respond.*)

DAPHNE: So there's this…odd…

MICHAEL: Actually I'm very close with my parents.

DAPHNE: Yeah.

MICHAEL: I visit my dad. He's gotten it together.

DAPHNE: Right.

MICHAEL: I laugh with his wife. I tickle their babies.

DAPHNE: Right.

MICHAEL: I drop in on mom. Say hi to her husband. Keep up with his kids. Say hi to my brothers.

DAPHNE: Yeah.

MICHAEL: I'm back in touch with mom's ex. My sister stays in his basement.

DAPHNE: Uh huh. But I mean, this sort of—

MICHAEL: I'm very close with this planet too.

DAPHNE: Right.

MICHAEL: Air. Water. Great location.

DAPHNE: Right.

MICHAEL: Me and my planet, two heaps of shit going in circles.

DAPHNE: But moving in here, you feel this sort of—

(*A sudden sound from inside the bedroom.*)

DAPHNE: You know because it's all so—

(*From the bedroom, sounds of bed rocking. Gasps, groans, grunts. Silence*)

DAPHNE: It's all sort of—

(COURTNEY *rushes out, wrapped in towel, hurries through living room and out main door [to the bathroom]. Sound of running water.*)

DAPHNE: I…

(DOUG *rushes out, wrapped in towel, hurries through living room and out main door [to the bathroom]. Sound of running water.*)

DAPHNE: I…

(COURTNEY *charges back through main door, into bedroom, closing doors behind her.*)

(DOUG *charges back through main door, into bedroom, closing doors behind him.*)

(DAPHNE *charges into closet.*)

(MICHAEL *sits there.*)

(DOUG *comes out from the bedroom, disheveled, despondent, closes the door behind him, sits.*)

DOUG: No one here knows my high school hike club scaled four peaks, I led the way, I won a prize. No one here knows I sprained my foot in a snake pit, kept right on going, everybody cheered and elected me president. No one here knows the feeling, your boots in the dirt, your face in the wind, your picture in the paper. What a gang, what a time, no one knows.

MICHAEL: About ready to head to the picnic?

DOUG: I might have a prior commitment.

MICHAEL: If you had a prior commitment, you'd already know.

DOUG: She'll be right out, to let me know.

MICHAEL: If you want her to want you, don't let her catch you waiting for her.

DOUG: (*Looks to the bedroom door, thinks*) Huh.

MICHAEL: You might also want to go for some deodorant.

DOUG: I go for plenty of deodorant.

MICHAEL: Go for more.

DOUG: *(Sniffs himself, thinks)* Huh.

MICHAEL: Let's head up to the room. I'll do course cards, you call about your lab course…

DOUG: Why are you telling me to call about my lab course.

MICHAEL: To see if you're in.

DOUG: I did see. I'm…almost in.

MICHAEL: Almost in?

DOUG: If someone drops out, I'm in.

MICHAEL: Oh.

DOUG: *(Suddenly incensed)* Excuse me but I'm proud of being almost in? Okay "almost in" is a key step towards being in? Okay I'm sorry I'm not as "in" as you think humanly necessary but not everybody was born into a nationally ranked program that basically guarantees advanced standing?, but at least I'm sticking out my neck instead of dreaming about some graduate level seminar while fiddling with my god damn course cards? *(He charges out the main door.)*

(DAPHNE steps out from the closet.)

DAPHNE: *(To MICHAEL)* I'm heading out if you want to come…

(COURTNEY comes out of the bedroom.)

COURTNEY: If I joined you two, would that be okay?

DAPHNE: Might it not be not okay for you?

COURTNEY: It'll be great for me, as long as it's okay with you.

DAPHNE: But, might you not, see something better, and feel tied?

COURTNEY: No.

DAPHNE: But aren't you always keeping an eye out, for, you know, whatever, whatever else?

COURTNEY: When things happen, things happen, but, I never lose sight of my friends. How can you say that.

DAPHNE: I meant that crate to be for my books, so why is it covered with your candles?

COURTNEY: When you tacitly approve of someone's candles on your crate while secretly resenting them, you're not doing the person a favor.

(DOUG *enters with flowers.*)

DOUG: *(To* COURTNEY*)* What was I doing standing in the flowers being stared at like I was crazy by the people I'd been talking with almost happily til the wind shifted and filled me with this feeling of your hair that swept fingers to flowers and feet to stairs to invite you to join me, please join me?

COURTNEY: I'm so sorry, but my roommate and I are in the middle of a conversation.

DAPHNE: *(To* MICHAEL*)* Weren't *we* in the middle of a conversation?

DOUG: Where's the god damned iced tea.

COURTNEY: It's empty.

DOUG: I want another crack at it, just one more crack.

COURTNEY: I'm sorry.

(A phone starts ringing.)

DOUG: I'll re-center your couch. I'll flip it around. I'll stand it on its legs.

COURTNEY: I'm sorry.

DOUG: *(On his back, beneath couch)* Did I only *dream* you wanted to go to the picnic with me? *(To* DAPHNE*)* If you had other plans what happened to them?

DAPHNE: *(Not moving)* I'm going to take a nap.

COURTNEY: *(To* MICHAEL*)* Have you any idea how absolutely rude it is to sit there, as though we're not worth one syllable of your divine wisdom?

*(*DAPHNE *answers her phone.)*

DAPHNE: Hello? *(Pause)* Right. *(Pause)* Right. *(Pause)* *(She hangs up.)*

DAPHNE: My father died.

(Everybody stands there.)

(Blackout)

END OF PLAY

LITTLE RED RIDING HOOD

Stage production rights licensed by Playscripts Inc.
This version is revised from earlier published one.

LITTLE RED RIDING HOOD premiered at the Fournos Centre for the Arts and New Technologies in Athens, Greece produced by Armadillo Theatre Group. It was featured in a triple bill of plays about adolescence, along with Euripides' IPHIGENEIA AT AULIS and Lee Breuer's RED BEADS. The cast and creative contributors were:

LITTLE RED RIDING HOOD .... Georgina Daliani
MOTHER .... Fotini Demiri
HUNTER .... Christos Rachiotis
WOLF .... Giorgos Basiakos
GRANDMOTHER .... Evangelia Andritsanou

Translator & director .... Evangelia Andritsanou
Set .... Constantinos Kypriotakis
Costumes .... Natalia Makrygianni
Choreography .... Sylvia Vousoura
Music .... Michalis Moustakis
Lighting .... Alekos Anastasiou

CHARACTERS

LITTLE RED RIDING HOOD
MOTHER
HUNTER
WOLF
GRANDMOTHER

Scene 1

(LITTLE RED RIDING HOOD *and her* MOTHER.)

MOTHER: This fresh fruit pie should help make grandmom strong again, don't you think Red?

RED: Yes mother.

MOTHER: Let's add a warm muffin for the woman who made my bed and kissed me good night.

RED: Yes mother.

MOTHER: Let's stuff the muffin with a stone so she'll choke.

RED: Yes mother.

MOTHER: That woman said I was worthless, Red.

RED: I understand, mother.

MOTHER: When she chokes force this wine between her lips 'til she gags.

RED: Yes mother.

MOTHER: She banged my head against a cupboard.

RED: I understand.

MOTHER: But she sure could soothe me to sleep with a bed time story. So lean grandmom forward and pat her back 'til she coughs up the stone.

RED: Yes mother.

MOTHER: Apologize to the woman who gave birth to your mother.

RED: Yes mother.

MOTHER: Then smash her head with a chair.

RED: Yes mother.

MOTHER: On second thought, it would be a shame to smash grandmom when she's already suffering so. Let's wait 'til she's feeling better to choke her and smash her. For now just bring her the goodies.

RED: Yes mother.

MOTHER: Stay on the open path the whole way, don't wander into the woods.

RED: I won't mother.

MOTHER: If a stranger pokes his head out ignore him.

RED: I will mother.

MOTHER: Move in a smooth steady step and he won't even notice you.

RED: I will.

MOTHER: Eyes ahead. Face down. What's that ugly frown? We're talking about keeping the stranger at a distance, not disgusting him.

RED: All right mother.

MOTHER: If he smells like a toad he's a king. Kiss his lips.

RED: I will mother.

MOTHER: Don't suck his tongue or he'll turn into a dwarf who'll haul you to his hovel and you'll never be heard from again.

RED: I understand.

MOTHER: If he tries to touch you scream.

RED: I will.

MOTHER: If he doesn't try to touch you put his hand on your breast.

RED: I will.

MOTHER: If he enjoys touching you he's a hideous gnome. Run like crazy.

RED: I will.

MOTHER: If he charms you he's a prince. Stab him to death.

RED: I will mother.

MOTHER: Stab him right to death or he'll carry you to his castle and you'll never be heard from again.

RED: I will mother.

MOTHER: Unless he's a handsome prince.

RED: Okay.

MOTHER: In that case ignore him completely so he'll follow you forever.

RED: I will.

MOTHER: What are we saying. You're too young to talk to strangers. Go straight to grandmom's.

RED: Bye bye.

MOTHER: You're going?

RED: To grandmom's.

MOTHER: How dare you desert me?

RED: Sorry mother.

MOTHER: You'll stay? Oh wonderful. Help me with my chores?

RED: All right mother.

MOTHER: First, take these goodies to your grandmother's.

RED: All right mother.

MOTHER: Wait. There are dangers out there. Not if she stays on the path. But if she strays from the path. She might stray from the path. Get back here.

RED: All right.

MOTHER: Don't cling to your mother.

RED: All right.

MOTHER: Sit down, I'm talking to you.

RED: All right mother.

MOTHER: It's a beautiful day. Get some sunshine.

RED: Okay.

MOTHER: Better yet, run these goodies over to your grandmother's.

RED: I will. *(She exits.)*

MOTHER: I knew one day she'd leave.

Scene 2

(RED *and* THE BIG BAD WOLF)

WOLF: Nice hat. You from around here?

RED: Yeah.

WOLF: It's a pretty area.

RED: Your woods seem nice.

WOLF: Much cooler.

RED: Don't get much light I guess.

WOLF: Less light. Lots of space. Good location.

RED: It is.

WOLF: Fine view.

RED: You call it woods or wood?

WOLF: Woods, wood, forest…

RED: Both.

WOLF: Don't ask me what a thicket is.
Come sit in the shade.

RED: No thanks.

WOLF: I like your basket.

RED: It's my mom's.

WOLF: Can I see?

RED: I have to get to my grandmother's.

WOLF: That's your grandmother?

RED: You know her?

WOLF: Down at the end of the road, right at the fork—

RED: Left—

WOLF: Yeah, left, til you pass the lake—

RED: Right before the lake.

WOLF: That place. Right. Sweet woman.

RED: She's been sick.

WOLF: She has seemed kind of…unwell.

RED: Does your face sweat a lot?

WOLF: No more than yours.

RED: How far out do your claws come?

WOLF: Tah dah.

RED: Gleaming needles.

WOLF: I keep them clean.

RED: They're so long.

WOLF: Thank you.

RED: I've never seen such big teeth.

WOLF: I've never seen such smooth bare hands. How
do you keep them so smooth?

RED: I don't know. *(She slaps her ankle.)* Mosquito.

WOLF: I'll scratch it for you.

RED: No thanks.

WOLF: It's the least I can do. You wouldn't have been bitten if you hadn't stopped to talk with me.

RED: Somebody scratching somebody else's bite?

WOLF: When you scratch yourself you can't fully enjoy the relief. Let me have your leg. Come on. Pull up. Up, I don't want to tear anything. Slide down the sock. Relax.

RED: Ow. Ee. Uh.

WOLF: Now with the teeth.

RED: Ooo—Stop. Someone could see. What would…

WOLF: You're right.

RED: So.

WOLF: The itch is gone, right?

RED: Just a little dot of blood.

WOLF: Are you feeling warm?

RED: No.

WOLF: There are little beads of sweat on your forehead.

RED: That's the way it goes.

WOLF: So how about a tour of the woods?

RED: Oh no.

WOLF: You're sure?

RED: I have to get to grandmom's house.

WOLF: I should be going too. But let me give you some advice. You walk too fast. Take some time to admire the beautiful flowers along the path. Pick your grandmother a bouquet.

(WOLF *goes.* RED *plucks flowers.*)

RED: Staring at the sun. Sobbing little drops. Pluck.
Gripping the dirt. Soft little stem. Pluck. Whispering?
Shh. Pluck. Pluck. *(Swept away, until breathless)* Blue.
Pluck. Purple. Pluck. Pink. Pluck. Pluck. Pluck. Pluck.
Pluck. Pluck.

Scene 3

(The HUNTER *sits, is served by the* MOTHER. *One of the
Hunter's arms is outside the sleeve of his shirt.)*

HUNTER: Where's my steak and eggs.

MOTHER: Coming dear.

HUNTER: If a hunter doesn't have his steak and eggs he
can't grab his gun and if he can't grab his gun he can't
blast the beasts and if he can't blast the beasts how's he
gonna market their meats if he can't market their meats
there's no way he can house his spouse and if he can't
house his spouse then where's he supposed to eat his
steak and eggs, in the god damn mud crap slop?

MOTHER: You didn't get one of your arms into your
shirt, dear.

HUNTER: Sure you miss a sleeve now and then or
sometimes you forget to button a few buttons, but
what about the sleeve you did get into the shirt, what
about the buttons you did button. I'm sick and tired of
people who always focus on the empty sleeve or the
unbuttoned button—

MOTHER: Your fly's open.

HUNTER: —or the opened fly, when the fact is,
when push comes to shove, it's the people with the
unbuttoned buttons and unsleeved arms who are out
there not looking at the people who are looking at

them but just plain out there being out there. I'm out there.

MOTHER: I know you're out there, dear.

HUNTER: I'm the one who faces the heat and the dirt and the stink and the slime, and let me tell you it gets filthy and sweaty out there in the heat, but I never back down from the filth or run away from the slime, I stand right up to the smelly boiling stinking filth and why? So I can shoot the beasts that make the coats that cover the backs of the very people who stand there staring at my empty sleeve when they should have been paying more attention to the arm in their own back yard in the first place.

(HUNTER *struggles to slide his arm into his sleeve while using the other hand to eat.*)

MOTHER: It'd be easier to get your arm in if—

HUNTER: Easy sure, easy is good, easy is nice, everybody wants easy, but let me tell you sister sometimes somebody has to stand up and go out and get out and stand up and get up and get out and go out and rrrr rrr rrrrrr rrrrrrr— (*As he wrestles with the shirt he sticks his leg through the chair.*)

MOTHER: You're tangled up in the chair, dear.

HUNTER: Of course there'll be a few tangled chairs along the way. A night in hell is no picnic. (*While wrestling with the chair he bangs his head against the table.*)

MOTHER: You banged your forehead on the table.

HUNTER: You're damn straight there are gonna be a few heads banged on a handful of tables, but you can rest assured that when I feel the fresh air in my lungs I'll be thanking God I live in a house where I have the right to shove my foot through a chair and bang my head on a table—

MOTHER: Watch out for the fork.

HUNTER: —and ram my face with a fork if I want to so I can go out and get my family a sack of juicy steaks.

MOTHER: You chipped the plate.

HUNTER: And a plate.

MOTHER: And a chair.

HUNTER: And a chair.

MOTHER: And some eggs.

HUNTER: Did you make a list?

MOTHER: See you at supper.

(HUNTER *exits.* MOTHER *shakes her head and smiles.*)

Scene 4

(GRANDMOTHER *in her bed.*)

GRANDMOTHER: Yecch. *(Spits)* I'm spitting up my rotten guts. Where's my lousy bowl. Have to crawl to the cupboard on my throbbing knees. Can't open the latch with my cracked up knuckles. Back to the bed for that worthless ointment. Can't grip the cap in my rotten wrecked up teeth, where's my busted tweezers. Lousy bowl was right here the whole time. Useless eyes. Yecch. *(Spits)* Missed.

(A knock at the door)

GRANDMOTHER: Knock knock yourself.

WOLF: It's Little Red Riding Hood with a snack from mother.

GRANDMOTHER: Couldn't keep down a snack if I wanted to.

WOLF: There's a pie and a muffin...

GRANDMOTHER: Leave me alone.

WOLF: and some wine…

GRANDMOTHER: Come in.

(WOLF *enters.*)

WOLF: Into the closet. I'm here to eat your granddaughter.

GRANDMOTHER: What's wrong with me?

WOLF: I'll eat you later.

GRANDMOTHER: Right now or I don't budge.

WOLF: Sorry but I'm going to relax now to get ready for Little Red.

GRANDMOTHER: You could put an end to every ache in my body in three seconds and I demand you do it.

WOLF: I'm a wolf, not a social worker. I'll get to you when I feel like it.

GRANDMOTHER: You'll never eat me, I know it. I'll keep getting more dumb and decrepit til there isn't a tooth left in my—ocean? teaspoon? and I can't even get myself up out of the—soldier? celery? —Oh stitch. I'm losing my ability to plant. I can hardly pair. Please shove me into your three and cloud me. Chew my worthless green and my aching was and my throbbing hilltop into a thousand guppy candle. This is knife. Look at my tree. Are you glorious? Blades are streaming down my sun and it's all because you won't rip head run your salt worm eye. I'm rubbing on my bended ship.

WOLF: Old ladies are a pain in my ass. Okay, I'll eat you if—

GRANDMOTHER: Huh?

WOLF: I'll eat you—

GRANDMOTHER: What?

WOLF: I'll—

GRANDMOTHER: Now I can hardly hear a word you flay. There's just this loud table. I'm losing my fish. I'm going scratch.

WOLF: *(Into her ear)* I'll eat you if you hand me your shawl.

GRANDMOTHER: *(Relieved)* The. Is. A.

(GRANDMOTHER hands WOLF her shawl, crawls under the sheets. He crawls under, eats her, emerges in her shawl.)

Scene 5

(RED and the WOLF.)

RED: Grandmom?

WOLF: Come on in honey. Shut the door. Get comfy. Surprise.

RED: Hi.

WOLF: Hi.

RED: How've you been?

WOLF: Thinking about you. How have you been?

RED: Since grandmom's gone we can have a muffin.

WOLF: I would love a muffin.

RED: Okay.

WOLF: How'd it get smushed?

RED: My mother put a stone in and took it out again.

WOLF: Why'd she do that?
Anyway, it's a delicious muffin.

RED: You looked weird in grandmom's shawl.

WOLF: Did I surprise you?

RED: No.

WOLF: I was afraid if you saw me right when you walked in you might run away. You seemed shy before.

RED: I picked flowers like you said.

WOLF: Very nice.

RED: You like this place?

WOLF: Nice light. I live in a hole. What?

RED: Huh?

WOLF: I thought you were going to say something.

RED: Oh no.
When I'm in your stomach will I be alive?

WOLF: You'll be unconscious.

RED: For how long?

WOLF: A few minutes. Then you run out of air. But you won't feel anything at that point.

RED: No one's woken up and couldn't breathe?

WOLF: Not that I know of.

RED: Couldn't you kill me with your teeth on the way in?

WOLF: It's better for me if I swallow you whole. And for you too. Less mess.

RED: Should I get undressed?

WOLF: Just take off your shoes.

RED: How was grandmom?

WOLF: I prefer kids.

RED: On the bed?

WOLF: Sure.

(RED *and* WOLF *go to the bed.*)

WOLF: I really do like that hat.

RED: I'm now scared.

WOLF: Don't be.

(WOLF *eats* RED, *falls asleep.*)

Scene 6

(HUNTER *enters followed by the* MOTHER.)

MOTHER: She always comes straight home.

HUNTER: Would you shut the hell up with your senseless panic? See? There's her basket and her shoes and the wolf. Help. Wolf. Help.

MOTHER: You've got a gun dear, he doesn't have a gun. And besides he's fast asleep.

HUNTER: Whoa. I'm in the perfect position to kill the biggest beast in the forest.

MOTHER: Let me cut Little Red from his belly first…

(MOTHER *pulls* GRANDMOTHER *and* RED *from the Wolf's belly.*)

HUNTER: I'm about to kill the Big Bad Wolf. Oh yes. Oh good.

MOTHER: You were in there too, Mother?

GRANDMOTHER: Uh guh duh buh.

HUNTER: (*Aims at the* WOLF) Ten. Nine.

MOTHER: She's lost her mind, Red. Should we scream?

RED: I don't know.

(GRANDMOTHER *gags, writhes.*)

HUNTER: Eight. Seven.

MOTHER: It happens to everyone.

HUNTER: Six.

RED: I want…

HUNTER: Five.

RED: ...the Wolf.

HUNTER: Four.

MOTHER: What?

HUNTER: Three.

MOTHER: You want...

HUNTER: Two.

MOTHER: The Wolf?

HUNTER: She wants the Wolf?

MOTHER: Talk to her.

HUNTER: I'm about to shoot the Wolf.

MOTHER: You can't shoot the Wolf 'til you've talked to her.

HUNTER: Listen, young lady. You are a piece of God.

MOTHER: That means nothing to her.

HUNTER: Listen, young lady. You are a piece of fish.

MOTHER: What he means is—

HUNTER: No one knows what you are.

MOTHER: He's saying that—

HUNTER: A life unlived is a terrible thing to lack.

MOTHER: He means—

HUNTER: You have what you are, but you get what you make.

MOTHER: Although now you feel ugly and stupid—

HUNTER: Your mother's right.

MOTHER: —rest assured that I've been there dear,

HUNTER: Your mother's right.

MOTHER: And it will get better.

HUNTER: Your mother's right.

MOTHER: It'll never be easy.

HUNTER: She's right.

MOTHER: But it'll always be full.

HUNTER: She's right.

MOTHER: Of shit.

HUNTER: She's right.

MOTHER: But one day you'll realize—

HUNTER: What your mother's trying to say is life's filled with pitfalls but with every stormy sea your spirit grows stronger and stronger and stronger and stronger—*(Continues as* MOTHER *speaks)* and stronger and stronger and stronger and stronger and

MOTHER: *(During the above)* And one day someone will come along and you'll know that you'll always be sure deep inside that—

(GRANDMOTHER *screams silently.)*

MOTHER: Shut up.

HUNTER: Really.

MOTHER: Listen, Red. Life is good. The wolf is bad.

HUNTER: Hold your ears, ladies. *(He shoots several times until the stage is filled with smoke.)* Got him. Probably.

Scene 7

(RED *holds onto* WOLF's *legs.)*

RED: Please eat me again Mister Wolf. I'll just curl into a little ball and slide right down. Let me in, please please?

WOLF: I can't eat you. I'm dead. So I've really got to be moving on.

RED: Eat me first?

WOLF: It's too late. I'm sorry.

RED: It's not fair.

WOLF: Tell me about it.

RED: My arms want you and my knees want you and my bones want you.

WOLF: I wanted you too. Very much. But I can't help you now. Let go.

RED: So what do I do.

WOLF: Live happily ever after I guess.

RED: Huh.

END OF PLAY

NEGOTIATION

NEGOTIATION premiered at the U S Comedy Arts Festival in Aspen Colorado in 1997. The cast and creative contributor were:

EMPLOYER ....Kelly Connel
FREELANCER..Mark Grapey
Director...Michael Patrick King

The play was subsequently performed in New York at M C C. The cast and creative contributor were:

EMPLOYER ....Matthew Lewis
FREELANCER...................................... Christopher McCann
Director...Evan Handler

CHARACTERS

Employer
Freelancer

(EMPLOYER *sits behind a desk,* FREELANCER *sits in a chair.*)

EMPLOYER: How much could you do the job for?

FREELANCER: What were you planning to spend?

EMPLOYER: What would you normally charge?

FREELANCER: I can work around your figure.

EMPLOYER: Give me a number.

FREELANCER: I could do the whole thing for, probably, twenty-five.

EMPLOYER: We can't pay anything like that.

FREELANCER: I could swing it for fifteen.

EMPLOYER: Sorry but

(*Simultaneously:*)

EMPLOYER: I'm not authorized to go over twelve thousand.

FREELANCER: I couldn't afford to go under twelve hundred.

EMPLOYER: You were talking hundreds?

FREELANCER: You were talking thousands?

EMPLOYER: Twelve hundred would be fine.

FREELANCER: When I said twelve hundred, I was just tossing out twelve hundred as a ballpark number, that I could take up front, as long as my total came to at least twelve thousand.

EMPLOYER: When I said twelve thousand, I meant the annual budget that I'm working within, since with all of the cut-backs, I'm stuck handling this whole project with a total of twelve hundred.

FREELANCER: I could approach it for seven thousand.

EMPLOYER: I couldn't possibly go above two.

FREELANCER: I'd be taking a loss below six.

EMPLOYER: I could dig up three if you'll start tomorrow.

FREELANCER: I'll start tomorrow for five.

EMPLOYER: I'll see if I can get you four.

FREELANCER: That's low for me, and it's the busy season, and another client is breathing down my neck…

EMPLOYER: I'll pay you under the table.

FREELANCER: Deal.

EMPLOYER: I like your stuff. You'll get half your total fee after each dozen transplants.

FREELANCER: Transplants?

EMPLOYER: You *do* do heart transplants?

FREELANCER: No, I'm a painter. I paint houses.

EMPLOYER: I see.

FREELANCER: I'd feel a little silly accepting four thousand under the expectation that I should perform two dozen heart transplants.

EMPLOYER: Five thousand.

FREELANCER: What am I supposed to do, stay up all night reading medical books and watching instructional videos and practicing on toads?

EMPLOYER: Six thousand.

FREELANCER: Under the table?

EMPLOYER: Deal. You've got what it takes. I'll get you the first thousand candy bars now.

FREELANCER: Candy bars?

EMPLOYER: We pay for all transplants in candy bars.

FREELANCER: I work for dollars, not candy bars.

EMPLOYER: Candy bars are more than a dollar in some states.

FREELANCER: I'm not going to stay up all night learning how to perform heart transplants for six thousand candy bars.

EMPLOYER: Seven thousand.

FREELANCER: Listen. It's one thing for us to sit here and talk about me becoming a competent heart surgeon over night, but I think we both know that in reality I'm bound to botch a few incisions and get blood all over the place and kill a few people and get clobbered by angry relatives and wind up in jail.

EMPLOYER: Eight thousand.

FREELANCER: I have no place to put eight thousand candy bars.

EMPLOYER: Nine thousand.

EMPLOYER: I'd break out in pimples.

EMPLOYER: Nine fifty.

FREELANCER: I'd throw up all over.

EMPLOYER: Nine ninety.

FREELANCER: They'd melt, there'd be flies…

EMPLOYER: Ten thousand.

FREELANCER: Deal.

EMPLOYER: You're quite a person.

FREELANCER: I'm not a person, I'm a gorilla. See?
(Exposes furry belly)

EMPLOYER: I'm sorry, hiring a relatively inexperienced human is one thing, but this job is far too delicate for a gorilla.

FREELANCER: I'll do all twenty-four transplants for a single squashed candy bar.

EMPLOYER: All right, but only if you'll be my one true love.

FREELANCER: Under the table?

EMPLOYER: Deal.

*(*EMPLOYER *and* FREELANCER *go under the table.)*

END OF PLAY

GUILT

GUILT premiered at the Actors Theatre of Louisville in April, 2003. The cast and creative contributors were:

DIDI .... Valerie Chandler
BIG GUY .... Justin Tolley
THIN MAN .... Daniel Evans
MAXINE ....Bobbi Lynne Scott

Director .... Tanya Palmer
Set .... Brenda Ellias
Costumes ....Andrea Scott
Lighting ....Hillery Makatura
Sound ....Ben Marcum
Props ....Tracey Rainey & Ann Marie Werner
Stage manager ....Mary Ellen Riehl
Dramaturg ....Claire Cox

CHARACTERS

DIDI
BIG GUY
THIN MAN
MAXINE

(*Four chairs.* BIG GUY, MAXINE, *and* THIN MAN, *wear pajamas, sit very still.* DIDI *wears black dress, moves around.*)

DIDI: What happened. And who did it. I need to know.

(*The seated three stay still.*)

DIDI: I know it's late. And I'm sorry. But we need to talk about it. Now.

(*The three stay still.*)

DIDI: We all know it happened. We know that, right?

(*The three stay still.*)

DIDI: We're not pretending nothing happened, are we?

(*The three stay still.*)

DIDI: Are we sitting here and hoping? Is that what we're doing? Like if we don't say anything it never happened, it'll just go away?

(*The three stay still.*)

DIDI: What did we say about responsibility? About being adults? What makes us adults?

(*The three stay still.*)

DIDI: We're adults. Right?

(*The three stay still.*)

DIDI: Why. Why are we adults.

(*The three stay still.*)

DIDI: What makes us adults.

(The three stay still.)

DIDI: Adults are people who…

BIG GUY: They always close the door when they're on the toilet.

DIDI: We, not they. We're all adults, right?

BIG GUY: They always say How are you. How are you. How're *you*.

DIDI: That's right, because—

BIG GUY: They don't let their hands go all over the place when they're talking or if they move their hands it's only when they're Saying Certain Things.

DIDI: Okay…

BIG GUY: They don't—

DIDI: You keep saying They. You're an adult.

BIG GUY: They don't—

DIDI: We.

BIG GUY: They don't—

DIDI: You're an adult. Say We.

BIG GUY: We.

DIDI: Good.

BIG GUY: They don't rub their privates on things. They don't put their hands into their mouth. If they have to laugh when you're talking they don't just laugh they wait til you're done and then they laugh.

DIDI: Because we're considerate, right? Because, as adults, we're aware, of the other people. What they're feeling. And if we harm someone, we speak up.

THIN MAN: You can be in a room with like fifteen people. And you can tell what they're expecting, what they need to hear you say. You can anticipate their expectations. There's like a rhythm going on.

DIDI: You mean, at a party?

THIN MAN: You're surrounded with expectations but you're working within that. Who knows who from where, who wants you to say what. How to adjust your meaning, how to handle a silence, or like if there's somebody you want to get in with, how to take whatever phrase comes at you and spin it a certain way so in the blink of an eye you're— *(A fit of panting)* you're smack in the middle of the person's— *(Violent panting)*

DIDI: There's a breeze, it's swirling all around you, a cool breeze.

(THIN MAN stops panting, sits calmly.)

THIN MAN: You're in the middle of the person's affections.

DIDI: Well, you're talking about how we're able to connect to one another, and you're right, we are connected. And if we do something that disrupts, that affects the whole community, we can't curl up inside a shell. Right? We have to, what. We have to speak up.

MAXINE: I went out by myself.

(DIDI waits.)

DIDI: Uh huh.

MAXINE: I took a shower and I went out by myself.

(DIDI waits.)

DIDI: Does this have to do with—

MAXINE: I took. This morning. I took a shower. I took a shower. A shh…I took a shower and I went out by myself. I went out by myself.

(DIDI waits.)

DIDI: Does this relate to what we were talking about? *(She waits.)*

MAXINE: I went out.

(DIDI waits.)

DIDI: This is obviously very important to you, and we'll talk about it later, but right now we need to talk about how someone was killed.

(The seated three stay still.)

DIDI: It's a scary word, I know. And it's sad. It's very sad, but we need to talk about it. Or it will be out of our hands, we'll lose control, of who we see every day, who we can be with—

THIN MAN: If you kill someone, you get killed.

DIDI: Sometimes.

THIN MAN: When somebody's killed, they kill the killer. That's the rule.

DIDI: But the details matter, don't they? How the killing happened. What the person who did the killing was thinking.

THIN MAN: They kill the killer. That's the rule.

DIDI: Well I hate that rule. And I don't accept it.

BIG GUY: I think it's good they kill the killer because that way the dying happens in pairs and nobody has to be alone.

DIDI: That's ridiculous.

(The seated three stay still.)

DIDI: Listen. There's not going to be any more killing. We're going to get to the bottom of this right now. We're going to take a trip. So close your eyes, everyone.

(THIN MAN starts panting.)

DIDI: *(To Thin Man)* You can bring your cool breeze along on the trip.

(BIG GUY *wrings his hands, whines softly.*)

DIDI: *(To BIG GUY)* You can bring your song. Okay?
Concentrate on your song.

BIG GUY: *(Spoken, not sung:)* La. La. La. Dah.

(THIN MAN *stops panting.* BIG GUY *stops wringing his
hands and whining. As* DIDI *speaks the others rock and
sway, losing themselves in the imagined journey.*)

DIDI: So we're drifting…drifting off…towards a spot…
that's sort of dark…but familiar…a small sore…that
you just have to touch… You're tumbling down…and
there you are. Where are your arms. What are they
doing. See exactly where you are at the moment it
happened.

THIN MAN: But what if it's the kind of thing you can't
ever see, even when you're in it.

DIDI: What do you mean?

THIN MAN: Like if somebody's talking, but then the
channel gets changed and you're way down the hall.

BIG GUY: La la.

THIN MAN: Or there's an arrangement of people, you
get all these thoughts, then the color's slipped out of
everything.

BIG GUY: La la.

THIN MAN: You can't tell one minute from the next.

BIG GUY: La. Dah.

THIN MAN: And you're looking at your hands feeling
lonely.

BIG GUY: La la. La la.

(MAXINE *stomps her feet.* BIG GUY *wrings his hands,
whines.*)

THIN MAN: It's got to do with the head, doesn't it.

DIDI: Go on.

THIN MAN: It can't happen unless it gets to the head, that's where it always happens. *(He places his hands on the sides of his head and stands up slowly.)* Somebody's hands were on my head.

DIDI: That's right.

(MAXINE leaps up and charges DIDI's empty chair, stops herself.)

DIDI: Don't stop.

(MAXINE spreads her arms like she's about to embrace the chair, charges right into it, shoves it all around the floor.)

DIDI: Good. Good.

(MAXINE sinks to her knees, BIG GUY springs up.)

BIG GUY: Someone was holding my body in her arms. And I was holding her body in my arms. And my eyes got wet. And she held me harder. And her eyes got wet. And she said I'm sorry. I'm very very sorry. And I knew she was leaving me. And I thought "This is how it is to be killed. I'm being killed."

DIDI: That's right. That's it. I killed you all.

(The three sit and stay still.)

DIDI: I kept seeing you struggling, and never getting better, and I couldn't take that, so I decided to quit. I wanted to tell you. But I didn't know, how to put it. So when you were resting, I went over to each of you, and held you, and walked out. I went far away and I got a new job. But I kept hearing you. In the sounds coming from a radiator.

(BIG GUY emits a short whine, sits still.)

DIDI: In the breath of the person across from me.

(THIN MAN pants for an instant, sits still.)

DIDI: Right now I'm at a party, aren't I. Yes. I'm at a party. The adults are saying How are you and laughing in wonderfully varied patterns. I'm listening to their stories. And I'm nodding. But I'm not with them. I'm with you. I'm seeing you, still struggling, still not getting anywhere, and I feel like you're dying, like I killed you. But we're all just born, with certain tools, and awful things strike, they just drop down, and some of us just get hit, and the rest of us just keep going. I can't change that. I can't save anyone. No one can save anyone. Why can't I accept that? Since I left you it's been twenty years. That's a life sentence. When will I be able to talk to the people who are actually in the room? *(She sits.)*

MAXINE: I took a shower. It was freezing cold. Outside. I walked by myself outside and it was freezing cold. I was walking. There was trucks and there was dogs. The steam coming out of the dogs. There was, coming out of my head, twigs. There was twigs coming out of my head. I was touching my head and there was twigs. There was twigs coming out of my head. The shower. It was the shower. I took a shower and I walked out. I had ice on my head. The ice was the twigs. That's what I was thinking. When they came out. When they took me back I was thinking. I have ice coming out of my head.

DIDI: So do I.

(DIDI sits still, thinking. MAXINE charges into her, hugs her. BIG GUY stands, hugs her. THIN MAN puts his hands on the sides of her head. All three stand, embracing DIDI, moving slightly, as she sits completely still looking out.)

END OF PLAY

BLEEP THIS BLEEP

BLEEP THIS BLEEP premiered in the fall of 2007 at the Hamner Theater (Boomie Pederson and Peter Coy, Artistic Directors) in Crozet, Virginia. The cast and creative contributors were:

COOKIE .... Rose Harper
CLAY ....Sean Chandler
FELICIA .... Clare McGurk
GARRY.. Bill Williamson

Director..Clinton A Johnston
Set & lighting .... J Taylor, Peter Coy, Larry Hugo
Boomie Pederson

CHARACTERS

CLAY *and* FELICIA, *20s, are contestants in a reality show.*

COOKIE *and* GARRY, *30s-50s, are entertainment newscasters*

(A table on which there's a plate with a piece of toast. Near the table are two chairs, and CLAY *and* FELICIA. COOKIE *and* GARRY *observe from chairs on separate sides.)*

FELICIA: You took a bite out of my toast.

CLAY: No I didn't.

FELICIA: Yes you did you did. You took a bite out of my toast. I can't believe it.

CLAY: I did not take a bite out of your toast okay so stop accusing me because I didn't.

FELICIA: I was all ready to eat my toast and there's this huge bite I can't believe you.

CLAY: I didn't eat your toast Felicia.

FELICIA: So how'd it happen then.

CLAY: How do I know.

FELICIA: You know because you did it, why won't you admit it.

CLAY: Maybe you took a bite out of your toast without thinking about it, like you were walking around and having some daydream or something and you picked it up and took a bite and put it down without thinking.

FELICIA: BullshBLEEP.

CLAY: What's bullshBLEEP is you jumping all over me when I didn't do a thing.

FELICIA: Yeah right.

CLAY: It is right.

FELICIA: Nobody else was anywhere near the table and you're standing right there. You are so guilty.

CLAY: Oh I get it, are you setting me up, is that what this is about?

FELICIA: What?

CLAY: You're trying to make it look like I'm lazy and I steal so you can get the million dollars. This is part of a strategy.

FELICIA: I don't have a strategy, Clay. I want my toast so I can eat it. That's my strategy. When there's a piece of food and it's mine and I'm all ready to eat I want to eat it. That's my strategy.

CLAY: You've had a strategy from day one and you know it. You're trying to get rid of me.

FELICIA: I'm not trying to get rid of you. That's so not what this is about.

CLAY: Why don't I believe you.

FELICIA: Look I'm not going to stand here and pretend like I wouldn't like a million dollars, who wouldn't. But that's absolutely not why I've been doing what I do from day one, I can't believe you'd say that. I came here to make friends and be independent and discover stuff and get closer to Christ and have a good time.

CLAY: So did I.

FELICIA: And I was really feeling good about my relationship with you because you're someone I can talk to and really be open with about my faith.

CLAY: Me too with you, me too.

FELICIA: Because usually when I talk about my faith people get all weird.

CLAY: I know.

FELICIA: They act like you're, I don't know—

CLAY: Brain dead.

FELICIA: I know right? and so you have to act like you're not what you are, but you and I share that so we can really talk, I feel like I can totally talk to you.

CLAY: Me too with you.

FELICIA: I've totally enjoyed my time here, I've had such great experiences and I realize how lucky we are to be here, I don't mean to gripe because we really are lucky.

CLAY: We are so lucky to be here. We can't ever forget that.

FELICIA: And with you in particular I feel lucky and great and all but then I pick up my toast and you've taken—

FELICIA: this huge bite and I just wanna—	CLAY: I didn't bite your frickin' piece of—

(A series of asides to the audience:)

FELICIA: What happened then was—

CLAY: It was so weird.

FELICIA: Really weird.

CLAY: I couldn't believe it was happening.

FELICIA: I mean I could feel it building up and all—

CLAY: She wanted it to happen all right.

FELICIA: Or maybe he planned it.

CLAY: I did not plan it.

FELICIA: I didn't even know it was happening til it was half over.

CLAY: It was just—

FELICIA: Totally—

CLAY: Insane.

FELICIA: From nowhere.

(Again addressing one another:)

FELICIA: —this huge bite   CLAY: I didn't bite your
and I just wanna—   frickin' piece of—

(CLAY and FELICIA charge each other and start tickling each other.)

GARRY: *(To CLAY)* So the thing with the toast.

CLAY: *(Taking a chair from the table, sitting near GARRY)* I have no idea, Garry.

COOKIE: *(To FELICIA)* You just looked down and—

FELICIA: *(Taking a chair from the table, sitting near COOKIE)* Well Cookie there was this bite.

GARRY: And she went ballistic.

CLAY: She totally did.

FELICIA: Well you know I mean—

GARRY: *(To FELICIA)* But you can see how he would think you were setting him up, right?

FELICIA: No…

GARRY: It was a piece of toast after all, right? That's what you were blowing up about. Toast.

FELICIA: Yeah but…

GARRY: Bread and butter, slightly charred. Right? We're talking about a burnt piece of bread.

COOKIE: But we've all been there, Garry. You've got your day lined up. Your toast's all buttered. The sky's gleaming and all your ducks are lined up, finally. Your life-choices are feeling just right. You've made it through that feeling that you're going nowhere, that things are just never going to add up for you. Just maybe you're through that, just maybe you're on the road. And you pick up your toast. And there's this big fat bite.

FELICIA: Yes.

COOKIE: And that whole feeling is wrecked.

FELICIA: Yes.

COOKIE: All your life-choices stink. Your whole day is down the tubes, and you just want to give the person responsible a sock in the mouth.

CLAY: But I didn't do it.

GARRY: He says—

FELICIA: He says a lotta things.

GARRY: Isn't it possible that you were daydreaming about your wonderful day…

FELICIA: No.

COOKIE: What *about* Clay's explanation.

FELICIA: Absolutely not.

COOKIE: You're sure you—

FELICIA: I was not daydreaming and I was not setting him up.

COOKIE: We all make plans, Felicia.

FELICIA: Of course I make plans but I did not have a strategy to get rid of him, we totally have this trust like I said, at least I thought.

GARRY: Which brings me to something I was going to ask about if I may.

CLAY: Uh.

GARRY: You said you could trust each other because you're Christian.

FELICIA: That was…

GARRY: You said you can talk about your faith. Everyone else makes you feel weird. "Brain dead" you said.

CLAY: Uh.

GARRY: But you feel comfortable with each other because you share your faith.

CLAY: We didn't—

FELICIA: We didn't mean it to sound like that.

COOKIE: But you see why he's asking, right?

FELICIA: Sure but...

COOKIE: Can you two be as close to people who don't share your faith as you are to each other?

FELICIA: Absolutely.

CLAY: Absolutely.

GARRY: Would you have a problem for example trusting someone who, like me—

FELICIA: Absolutely not.

CLAY: No.

GARRY: Because there are people of all different—

FELICIA: It absolutely doesn't matter.

CLAY: We were just saying.

FELICIA: It's a positive thing, if you share a faith, it's something you can build on, but it's not like if you don't have that, whatever people share, that's great too.

CLAY: Whatever you believe that's fine.

COOKIE: So whatever someone believes—

GARRY: It's not like someone is better in your eyes.

FELICIA: It absolutely doesn't matter.

CLAY: That's so not what we're about.

FELICIA: If we offended anybody we're sorry that's not what we meant.

CLAY: Not at all.

GARRY: Thanks for letting me clear the air about that, I just wanted to address that and I think we're all grateful that the air has been cleared.

COOKIE: Now about the tickling.

FELICIA: Oh gosh.

CLAY: Here we go.

GARRY: What was that about.

FELICIA: It was so totally nothing.

COOKIE: It sure looked like there was something going on with that. Clay?

CLAY: Just one of those things.

COOKIE: Yeah but coming on top of the toast, it sure took me by surprise.

FELICIA: It's one of those things, you know?

COOKIE: Was it coming from nowhere? Felicia?

FELICIA: Gosh.

COOKIE: Or was it coming from somewhere.

FELICIA: I…

CLAY: It…

COOKIE: It was coming from somewhere, right? You want to whisper where it was coming from? You want to whisper it? Just whisper.

FELICIA: You want me to whisper?

COOKIE: Come on and whisper.

GARRY: I can't BLEEPing believe this.

COOKIE: What.

GARRY: I was the one who was going to confront them about the tickling. BLEEP.

COOKIE: We both asked them about the toast and about the Christian thing…

GARRY: But I said I was going to do the tickling, I had an angle on that, the whole if-you're-sitting-around-half-naked-of-course-the-inevitable-happens, that's perfect for me, but you jumped in and ran with it and left me sitting there like a piece of BLEEP.

COOKIE: I remember you saying you wanted to press them about the tickling but it wasn't spelled out—

GARRY: Oh my god are you after my twelve point five share is that it?

COOKIE: What?

GARRY: You're after my twelve point five, that's what this is about, my god my BLEEPing god.

COOKIE: Look I'd like a twelve point five who wouldn't but I don't wake up in the morning thinking how can I cop your numbers.

GARRY: Oh Christ Cookie I have principals, I do not go around BLEEPing people the second I get the chance.

COOKIE: Neither do I.

GARRY: I know it's not fashionable to have principals.

COOKIE: Believe me I know.

GARRY: Everybody. The minute you turn around—

COOKIE: I couldn't live like that believe me.

GARRY: So then why the BLEEP did you break the tickling thing Cookie.

COOKIE: Okay you can stop laying your BLEEP on me because I sat back and let you have your way with the toast and with the Christian thing, you ripped that the hell out of my mouth—you did, don't BLEEP me, don't pull that BLEEP, you left me lapping at your heels like a BLEEPing BLEEP dog and so maybe I was a little over eager with the tickling but it hurts when you rub your twelve point five in my BLEEPing face.

GARRY: I'm sorry but that's sure how it looks.

COOKIE: Well it sure looks to me like you're trying to BLEEP me.

GARRY: Me BLEEP you?

COOKIE: You're making me out to be this total BLEEP so my numbers go to hell.

GARRY: The BLEEP I am.

COOKIE: You're going on like I'm making you totally miserable—

GARRY: I'm not miserable, I know I'm lucky to be doing what I'm doing.

COOKIE: You are lucky.

GARRY: We're both lucky.

COOKIE: People would kill to be where we are.

GARRY: We're as close to the stuff everybody wants to be close to as you can be. Who's closer than us? Nobody. It's a privilege, and I'm humbled and grateful, but when I have this perfect opportunity all lined up I don't expect to be cut off at the knees—

| GARRY: —and by someone | COOKIE: I did not cut you |
| I totally— | off at the— |

(A series of asides:)

GARRY: What happened then—

COOKIE: I did not see it coming.

FELICIA: Took me totally—

CLAY: From nowhere.

COOKIE: It had a history.

GARRY: I remember where I was standing.

FELICIA: One thing led to a—

CLAY: —rapid-fire.

COOKIE: My god I was—

GARRY: —blind-sided.

FELICIA: —blown away.

(To one another:)

GARRY: —and by someone   COOKIE: I did not cut you
I totally—   off at the—

*(COOKIE and GARRY grab hold of one another, struggle,
COOKIE falls towards CLAY and FELICIA, COOKIE grabs
onto CLAY who holds her up as she falls while FELICIA holds
onto CLAY.)*

GARRY: So Cookie's reaching out to you. And you grab
her, and you're holding her.

CLAY: She was falling.

GARRY: But you've got Felicia already there, right?

FELICIA: Yeah, Clay.

GARRY: Felicia's holding onto you, but you're clinging
to Cookie. Pressing firmly to Cookie and ignoring
Felicia, right?, to hell with Felicia?

CLAY: Cookie had this look on her face like—

GARRY: Okay so she gave you a look. Cookie gave you
a look. Did you give him a look, Cookie?

COOKIE: Oh come on Garry, we all know that feeling.
The panic of falling. Fear of twisting the ankle. Banging
the head on the ground. Getting the wind knocked
out of you. Lying there banged up, maybe bleeding.
Getting trampled and kicked. Nobody wants that. So
you reach out. It's a gut extinct.

CLAY: That's right.

GARRY: Excuse me, Clay, but why are you defending Cookie instead of—

COOKIE: Because when someone saves someone from falling there's a bond that's formed, Garry. It's a gut thing, holding and being held, all that sweat for a purpose. If you're hot it cools you down. If you're cold it warms you up. It feels good and it should and that's fine.

GARRY: But coming when it did, after this question about whether Cookie'd broken her agreement to let me confront you about the tickling—

FELICIA: Don't you get it Clay? She gets caught pulling a fast one on Garry and all of a sudden she's falling all over you? Doesn't it register that just maybe you're being used? Hello?

COOKIE: I did not "pull a fast one" or "fall all over" anybody.

CLAY: It looked to me like Garry pushed her.

GARRY: So you grabbed her and squeezed her and pressed her to your chest?

CLAY: She was falling.

FELICIA: What about me, Clay.

GARRY: What about Felicia.

FELICIA: I was off balance too, way up on the tips of my toes, the blood was rushing to my tippy toes and I was teetering.

CLAY: Yeah but—

FELICIA: You could smell my sweat and you could feel me teetering.

COOKIE: I'd already passed the point where I could support myself. I was going straight down.

FELICIA: You shoulda let her fall, Clay.

CLAY: I guess I knew Felicia was off balance but I saw Cookie falling first.

GARRY: So you've got this partner with whom you've built up this trust and then this other person reaches out to you from nowhere and that's worth an equal amount of your energy, strength and concern?

FELICIA: *(To* CLAY*)* I sure wish we were back at the table, just you me and the toast. Sure we'd bicker, but y'knew who was after what.

GARRY: Who is after what, Cookie. Who is after exactly what.

COOKIE: Shut the BLEEP up.

GARRY: Nobody knows any more, do they, because the floor's been ripped out from under us since the instant Cookie hurled herself at her little boy toy and sent the rest of us reeling through space.

CLAY: You're trying to get rid of me. Aren't you Garry.

GARRY: What?

FELICIA: What are you talking about, Clay.

CLAY: You're trying to make me look like I'm shallow and stupid.

GARRY: I'm shining a light on Cookie. A laser beam on Cookie. This isn't about me and you.

CLAY: Sure it is.

GARRY: I totally supported your version of the toast thing, didn't I Clay?

FELICIA: Where's this coming from, Clay?

CLAY: I guess I've been wondering, ever since he said about how he has principals.

FELICIA: He didn't mean anything by that.

CLAY: He jumped on us about our religion. Then he said stuff about principals like he has them but nobody else does, it's not "fashionable" he said.

GARRY: All I was saying is I have principals and some people don't have principals but there's nothing wrong with not having principals, respecting people without principals is one of my main principals, and by the way Cookie said it too and so—

COOKIE: I never accused other people of not having principals.

GARRY: The BLEEP you didn't.

COOKIE: The BLEEP I did.

CLAY: I guess I'm getting tired of your negative energy.

GARRY: Negative? I'm not being negative. I'm proud of where we are and thrilled with what we've got. Nobody's less negative than me. All I ever said was I have certain principals, and that works for me. But I can work with people who have religion, or people who have principals, or people who have religion *and* principals. Actually I come from a long line of people who had religion and *no* principals. Take my Uncle Jay and Aunt Sarah. Religion coming out their BLEEPs. But you sit at their dinner table and even mention a principal, one principal—

(CLAY *and* COOKIE *strangle* GARRY, FELICIA *joins in.*)

GARRY: *(Falling, to audience)* And it's happening to you is the thing 'cause your eyes and your mouth is still there but— *(He falls to the floor.)*

COOKIE: That was weird.

CLAY: It was weird.

FELICIA: It was like—

COOKIE: We were just—

CLAY: We did that but I mean—

FELICIA: I can't believe you guys.

CLAY: You did it too.

FELICIA: I wasn't going to but I thought if I sat back you'd team up against me.

CLAY: I had to get rid of him before he got rid of me.

FELICIA: Ever heard of voting somebody out?

CLAY: We're not at the table any more Felicia. You think if we took a vote he would have just walked away?

FELICIA: So you put your hands on his throat and squeezed until his eyes bulged and he was gasping for air?

COOKIE: If we waited Garry would have gone after Clay and then he could have picked off the rest of us one at a time. Remember how he got when I stepped on his toes with the talking about the tickling? And the way he jumped all over you with the religion thing? He would have never let that stuff drop. Believe me. I know Garry. Once he starts down a road…

FELICIA: So he wanted to get rid of us. Okay. So what about you, Cookie?

COOKIE: How could I get rid of anybody?

FELICIA: I don't know. Like maybe you're hiding something under those clothes?

CLAY: You are pretty covered up, Cookie.

FELICIA: We're wearing like nothing but she's got all these layers. What's that about.

COOKIE: If anybody should be worried here it's me because Clay is the only one strong enough to get rid of anybody and you two have that trust between you that goes way back.

CLAY: I think we'd all feel a little better if we could see what you've got under there.

COOKIE: I'm not about to undress in front of you guys.

CLAY: Why.

COOKIE: I'm just not comfortable doing that.

CLAY: Why.

FELICIA: Keep it together here Clay.

COOKIE: Because. I'm older than you. Nobody my age wants to undress in front of somebody your age. Trust me. There are things beneath these clothes that someone your age couldn't possibly understand.

CLAY: Sorry, Cookie. I can't take chances.

COOKIE: Okay, okay. You can feel me through my clothes. But that's it. And just certain, you know, regions.

(CLAY *starts over towards* COOKIE. FELICIA *follows behind.*)

FELICIA: Now Clay, just don't go and—

(CLAY *turns and strangles* FELICIA.)

FELICIA: *(Falling, to audience)* It's this feeling one minute you're— *(She falls.)*

COOKIE: The "feel me through my clothes" thing was weird, I know, but I had to get her off guard somehow, right?

CLAY: Right. So I got rid of Felicia because…

COOKIE: You and me have been teamed up ever since you kept me from falling, right?

CLAY: We have?

COOKIE: Sure we have. Right?

CLAY: So then, when you fell into my arms, you did that because you figured I'd stick with you and dump Felicia?

COOKIE: I knew you were open to getting rid of Felicia all along because if you'd been telling the truth about the toast you'd hate her for making it look like you were stealing and you'd want to get rid of her for that and if you'd been lying about the toast then that trust you guys had was an act and so when I realized Garry was after me and I figured I better get with someone else before it's too late you were the obvious choice because you guys obviously weren't working out plus you and I are natural partners because we both tend to not be the attackers, Felicia attacked you about the toast just like Garry attacked me about the talking about tickling but we both stood back while they did that and yes you attacked Garry and Felicia when they threatened you and I get the same way with my back to the wall, who doesn't, but we both generally prefer to sit back and take in this amazing situation that we're so lucky to be in instead of going around provoking people and barreling through to the end.

CLAY: Huh.

COOKIE: I can't tell you how great it feels to finally be able to sit back and—

(CLAY *strangles* COOKIE.)

COOKIE: *(Falling, to audience)* BLEEP.

(Cookie falls. Felicia, Cookie, Garry speak while down.)

FELICIA: Now I'm confused. Didn't you get rid of me because you and she were teamed up?

CLAY: I guess I only pretended like I was teamed up with her so I could get rid of her.

COOKIE: So then why did you get rid of Felicia?

CLAY: When Garry was gone I figured I could only be gotten rid of if the two women teamed up against me.

FELICIA: But why'd you get rid of me and not Cookie?

CLAY: I guess, looking down the road, I figured, I dunno, once I got rid of one of the women, I dunno…

COOKIE: The other would never be able to trust you.

CLAY: Yeah.

COOKIE: So you got rid of Felicia first because you thought you'd have a better chance of catching me off guard one-on-one.

CLAY: Yeah.

FELICIA: And then you got rid of her because it felt like you had to finish the job?

CLAY: Yeah.

COOKIE: So even though Felicia and me hadn't been on the same side of an issue except for those five seconds in the beginning when I supported her version of the toast thing you assumed we were this awesome inseparable team because we both have vaginas?

CLAY: Yeah.

FELICIA: Are you an idiot?

CLAY: No.

GARRY: So after I've been gotten rid of can I still compete?

COOKIE: (To FELICIA) We're together this time, right?

GARRY: If you two help me get rid of Clay I promise I'll never lie to you without telling you.

CLAY: You can't get rid of me. I got rid of you. It's not fair.

FELICIA: Oh Clay, the rules for breaking the rules aren't what they used to be. You poor BLEEP.

CLAY: Look I was totally open with everybody even when I was getting rid of them and I just did what I had to do which any of you would have done so I want my million dollars. Where's my million dollars. I want a million dollars.

(*The others close in on* CLAY, *he climbs onto the table.*)

CLAY: Someone give me a million dollars. It's time for my million dollars. I'm supposed to get a million dollars. I want my million dollars!

END OF PLAY

OF TWO MINDS

OF TWO MINDS premiered in Marathon 2003 at Ensemble Studio Theatre (Curt Dempster, Artistic Director). The cast and creative contributors were:

KATHY .... Geneva Carr
ELIZABETH .... Annie Campbell
TODD.. Ian Kesler
BUCK .... Brad Bellamy
MATT .... Connor White

Director .... Jamie Richards
Sets .... Jennifer Varbalow
Lights .... Greg MacPherson
Costumes .... Daniele Hollywood
Sound .... Rob Gould
Props .... Brooke Fulton

CHARACTERS

KATHY, *40*
ELIZABETH, *17*
TODD, *27*
MATT, *13*
BUCK, *50*

1. KATHY AND ELIZABETH

(ELIZABETH *sits on a pillow, writing in a notebook.* KATHY *sits in a chair, making pencil markings in a big book, never looking at* ELIZABETH.)

ELIZABETH: *(Taps her foot in rhythm)*

KATHY: *(Not looking)* Sh.

ELIZABETH: My foot can't touch the floor?

(KATHY *doesn't answer.*)

ELIZABETH: *(Taps foot again, softly)*

(KATHY *raises her forefinger)*

ELIZABETH: My toes can't touch the ground beneath my feet?

(KATHY *doesn't respond.*)

ELIZABETH: For my brain to work my body needs to move, Mom.

(KATHY *doesn't respond.*)

ELIZABETH: You're telling me I can't do what I need to do for my brain to function in the place that I live?

KATHY: Shhhhhh.

ELIZABETH: *(Softly)* Yes what you're doing is for your job but this is for school which is every bit as important to me as your work is to you or don't I exist.

(KATHY *doesn't respond.*)

ELIZABETH: *(Softly)* You're making no attempt to understand my internal necessities but I totally understand yours and I make adjustments without you even asking like when you're watching a show about a woman who's got nobody and you get really quiet. Or when you're lying alone on a Saturday night and you start to pet the little hairs on your arm. Or when you take the phone into your room and you come back out and your eyes are all red I totally understand that, I give you a clear path to the Kleenex, I allow you your personal style—

KATHY: *(Stops working, not looking up)* The time to talk was at dinner. Isn't that right Elizabeth.

(ELIZABETH is stunned.)

KATHY: At dinner I wanted to talk but you didn't. Why didn't you talk then, Elizabeth. Why.

(ELIZABETH stammers.)

KATHY: This is my only chance to get this done, so if you need to make your noises now you'll have to go into the bedroom. *(She resumes her work.)*

ELIZABETH: *(Still more softly)* Of course I didn't talk at dinner because that's forced conversation and all words are meaningless if they're dragged out of my face and how could you even threaten to send me into that bedroom where no human being could possibly think because the walls are like three feet apart I could suffocate my thoughts ricochet off the walls duh-duh-duh-duh-duh-duh-

(KATHY raises a finger, starts to point to bedroom.)

ELIZABETH: *(More softly)* —and I'm sorry you don't care for the sound of my body making contact with the floor but suppose I can't stand the sound of your nostrils sucking in air or the sight of your sweaty pores

why should I be the one who has to go into that high
security shit-hole of a—

(KATHY, *without looking, points to bedroom*)

(ELIZABETH *leaps up, silent scream*)

2. TODD AND ELIZABETH

(TODD *sits at a desk.* ELIZABETH *sits in a chair.*)

ELIZABETH: The character's morally justified, right?

TODD: Is she?

ELIZABETH: That's what I intended, when I wrote
it, that people would feel—I mean standing up to a
mother who treats her like that, is totally justified,
right?

TODD: Is it?

ELIZABETH: To take action in the face of that kind of,
psychic brutality, has to be for the best.

TODD: For whom.

ELIZABETH: For her, for everybody, because it's right,
she knows that it's right.

TODD: How.

ELIZABETH: Because, you just know sometimes,
you know? You see through the hypocrisy, you're
outraged and sick and the path becomes clear, like
Hamlet, there's the future, it's true and it's good, no
more talking, you take action, you do it and you don't
question. Right?

TODD: Is it r—

ELIZABETH: It is. I believe that it's right.

TODD: Right or wrong I found your character
compelling. So I gave you an A.

ELIZABETH: Wow. Mister Medley.

TODD: Ms. Thomson. Your writing…speaks to me.

ELIZABETH: Your writing totally inspires me. I know you said we'd never find anything you wrote but I did a search and I came up with that story about the guy in the tree shouting down at people.

TODD: That.

ELIZABETH: I don't know why you hide your stuff, it's so great, it's so real, I mean your character was on a mission, he knew exactly what he wanted, and he shouted it out, he didn't care who heard, it's liberating.

TODD: It's not liberating, it's lonely. To be shouting the most simple, obvious things about your experience of the world, but no one gets what you're saying. All they hear down there is nonsense. So you wave your arms and scream, you're stuck inside a bundle of flesh waving your arms, you want to fly away, to just leave this little earth behind, because no one will ever get you. No one will ever get anyone.

ELIZABETH: Wow.

TODD: You'll miss your bus.

ELIZABETH: Oh I was going to ask how long you'll be with us.

TODD: Just til Mister Nelson gets back.

ELIZABETH: So one day we'll show up and you won't be here.

(TODD *shrugs.*)

ELIZABETH: Anyway…

TODD: I'm sorry I didn't get to meet your mother on parent teacher night.

ELIZABETH: Oh she works some nights. And I never tell her about those things. And we have different last names so even when she does show up nobody knows she's my mother. So are you coming to the game Friday night?

TODD: I wasn't planning to.

ELIZABETH: There's a bake sale, a dance, it's a fun night.

TODD: I'll see if they need help.

ELIZABETH: Really?

TODD: Sure.

ELIZABETH: Yeah? Oh, the other thing…

(ELIZABETH *lurches towards* TODD, *hugs him, kisses him, he kisses her. They separate.*)

3. KATHY AND TODD

(KATHY *sits at a desk,* TODD *sits in a chair.*)

KATHY: Of course you can tell me. Todd. You're one of our very best proofreaders. If something's bothering you, I should know.

TODD: It happened at my other job—

KATHY: Stop. I should tell you, a lot of people here have other jobs. And why shouldn't they. But if they tell me they have another job, I'm required to put that in their file, and when it's time for raises the higher-ups do consider, long term commitment.

TODD: Sure.

KATHY: You were saying.

TODD: Could *anything* I say…go into a file?

KATHY: Oh no no only if there are certain, extreme personal tendencies, that could, down the road, lead to something. You understand.

TODD: Sure.

KATHY: Anyway…

TODD: Well. I had…a moment…where I…gave in.

KATHY: You gave in.

TODD: For a moment.

KATHY: I see.

TODD: And it's shaken me.

KATHY: Ah.

TODD: Because there was a time…when things got… confused.

KATHY: Oh.

TODD: Mm.

KATHY: And you don't want to, slip back, to that.

TODD: Mmm.

KATHY: Well first let me say, I won't tell a soul, about this thing that you, haven't said. And second, I'll keep an eye on your work, and on you, and I'm sure you'll be fine.

TODD: Thank you.

KATHY: I'm glad to help. You're one of our best. It's my job.

TODD: Of all the supervisors on twenty-two floors, you're the only one I can be open with.

(KATHY *looks away.* KATHY *and* TODD *sit there.*)

KATHY: You know what? Why don't you take my cell number just in case. (*Writes it down*)

TODD: Thanks.

KATHY: So if you suddenly, if I'm not here…

(KATHY *hands* TODD *the number. They sit there.*)

TODD: Who's that picture?

KATHY: My daughter. Well, the back of her head. When she sees me with the camera she runs.

TODD: How old? Given that she's yours she couldn't be more than seven.

KATHY: Good guess.

(KATHY *and* TODD *sit there.*)

TODD: We should go for coffee sometime.

KATHY: Coffee is good.

TODD: Good.

KATHY: Well actually coffee makes me jumpy.

TODD: How about wine.

KATHY: Wine is good. Or coffee.

TODD: Or we could go to a movie.

KATHY: A movie.

TODD: You don't like movies?

KATHY: Movies are good, sometimes. But sometimes they take a turn. The whole tone changes, the sound effects get really grating, the whole thing's going straight downhill and you're stuck there squirming in your seat.

TODD: Anyway.

(TODD *stands.* KATHY *stands. She hugs him. They hug. They kiss.*)

4. KATHY AND ELIZABETH

(ELIZABETH *and* KATHY *sit across from each other eating dinner.*)

KATHY: I heard you whistling last night.

ELIZABETH: Must have been a pipe.

KATHY: I know your whistling. Want to tell me what's up?

ELIZABETH: Sometimes I just whistle.

KATHY: At three A M?

ELIZABETH: I guess I was thinking, about Jenna. This guy she started up with, was supposed to meet up with her on Friday night, and he didn't show.

KATHY: Boys get scared.

ELIZABETH: He's not a boy. He's like, older.

KATHY: How much.

ELIZABETH: Significant amount.

KATHY: What's significant.

ELIZABETH: Half a generation. So it's weird.

KATHY: We can't all be the same age, Liz. He's not a different species. To encounter difference, that's why we get up in the morning.

ELIZABETH: Unless the age difference matters to the guy, and that's why he's avoiding her.

KATHY: If he avoids her without explaining then he's a jerk.

ELIZABETH: He is not.

KATHY: She doesn't need that.

ELIZABETH: I think he's got a lot on his mind.

KATHY: Abuse by any other name, Lizzie.

ELIZABETH: God. What's your problem.

KATHY: Sorry. I've been dealing with, Sue. She's going through a hard time.

ELIZABETH: I wondered why you'd go to the movies with her three Friday nights in a row.

KATHY: She's needed to talk, about this guy she's seeing who's younger.

ELIZABETH: How much.

KATHY: I don't know. Fifteen years.

ELIZABETH: He's fifteen years younger than she is?

KATHY: At most.

ELIZABETH: Won't last.

KATHY: Actually it's going great, basically. But she gets nervous because sometimes he's...puzzling.

ELIZABETH: She only sees him one night a weekend.

KATHY: How'd you know that.

ELIZABETH: Because she's gone out with you three Friday nights in a row, right?

KATHY: Well right. She does only see him one night a weekend.

ELIZABETH: If he's really into her he'd see her both nights.

KATHY: At our age you're glad to start slower.

ELIZABETH: He's not your age, he's fifteen years younger.

KATHY: Ten years tops.

ELIZABETH: He's going to dump her any minute.

KATHY: They're doing great did you hear me?, it's just the usual getting-to-know-each-other pains, you're not an authority on things you don't know.

ELIZABETH: *(Stops eating pudding)* You took my chocolate chips for your pudding.

KATHY: They were in the cupboard.

ELIZABETH: Way in the back.

KATHY: That's still the cupboard.

ELIZABETH: What was I supposed to do, tape them to the ceiling?

KATHY: I thought you'd like the surprise.

ELIZABETH: I buy those chips with my own money so I can take one handful of chocolate chips before bed every night.

KATHY: Liz.

ELIZABETH: It's my one minute of pleasure I look forward to all day. You saw my one pleasure and you stuffed it in your pudding.

KATHY: Lizzy.

ELIZABETH: The minute I trust you, you stab me in the back. I can't be in the same room as you.

KATHY: Well you'll have the place to yourself this weekend because I'll be away.

(Pause)

ELIZABETH: Good.

5. TODD AND MATT

(MATT lies on his belly, staring into a magazine, not looking at TODD.)

TODD: The Old Man will be here. He can sit outside your door as well as I can. Anyway, I'm only going away for the weekend—

(MATT screams softly.)

TODD: Look. I come and go. You know that. But the Old Man is reliable. Sure he's a pathetic piece of shit, but you can count on him. He married my mother and aggravated the hell out of her. Then he married your mother and aggravated the hell out of her. The man is a rock.

(MATT *says nothing.*)

TODD: He's a fine human being, really. We just have a special chemistry. He pushes my buttons so the sight of his face makes me vomit. But in reality he's harmless. So go to sleep.

(MATT *screams softly.*)

TODD: Is it that something'll happen to me, is that what you're scared of? Because whether I go out or not doesn't change the chances.

(MATT *doesn't respond.*)

TODD: Are you worrying about something happening to the Old Man?

(MATT *doesn't respond.*)

TODD: If anything happens to the Old Man you'll always have me. And if anything happens to me you'll have the Old Man. Whatever happens, we'll get through it. That's what family is. A bunch of demented maniacs who endure one another's company through disasters. So relax.

(MATT *doesn't respond.*)

TODD: *(Hears a sound)* He's here. If I slip out now I won't have to make eye contact. Sweet dreams.

(TODD *goes.* MATT *lies there, screams softly.*)

6. BUCK AND KATHY

(BUCK *and* KATHY *sit. She makes markings in her big book and shows them to him, who makes markings in his even bigger book.*)

BUCK: How could you not be feeling stress. All your people are feeling stress. So that funnels up to you.

KATHY: All the supervisors' stress must funnel up to you.

BUCK: My hands are shaking. Look. That's stress from work plus stress from home.

KATHY: Personal things?

BUCK: Not *my* home. That I leave at the door.

KATHY: Sure.

BUCK: But well, one of the other regional managers, who'll remain nameless, has been talking my ear off, about his son who, goes off.

KATHY: Ah.

BUCK: The son works for us—not this office, one of the others, and today—

KATHY: But it's against company policy to hire relatives, so how did...

BUCK: Nobody knows they're related, since the son grew up with his mother and keeps her husband's last name.

KATHY: Sure.

BUCK: So today the father dropped in on the branch office where the son works to say hi but his son walked right past him with this cruel blank expression and it really hurt me—to hear how much it hurt my friend, this other regional manager.

KATHY: That blank expression in the hallway. I hate it.

BUCK: Somebody does that to you?

KATHY: Not to me, to one of the other supervisors, who...let something happen, with a guy she supervises.

BUCK: That's a mistake.

KATHY: Tell me about it.

BUCK: So they carry on at work?

KATHY: Well no, he ignores her.

BUCK: Oh.

KATHY: And even outside of work he can't talk, about what he feels, where he's from, who he lives with, or where, he never invites her to his place.

BUCK: Weird.

KATHY: Is there somebody else? It's driving her nuts, she sees him constantly at work, he doesn't even look up, and it's really stressing me out—to keep seeing its affect on her.

BUCK: *(Rubs his lower back)* This much stress at my age is too much for my body.

KATHY: I've been waking up with a burning in my neck.

BUCK: Besides having the shakes my lower back pains are back.

KATHY: The burning shoots right up my spine.

BUCK: Take off your shoe. Really. What I heard works is, press the sole of your foot with your thumb, right in the center.

KATHY: *(Presses her foot)* Really?

BUCK: It's Chinese.

KATHY: For your lower back you do floor exercises, right?

BUCK: You hug your knee all the way in and breathe deep.

(KATHY *presses her foot while stretching up her neck.* BUCK *hugs his knee, breathes deep.)*

(KATHY *struggles to feel relief, searching, half faking, groans a bit.* BUCK *hugs both knees, grunts in pain.)*

(KATHY *begins to feel relief, sighs in pleasure.* BUCK *gets through the pain, grunts in pleasure.*)

(BUCK *and* KATHY *finish, relieved.*)

BUCK: Too bad we can't get them together.

KATHY: Your manager friend and my supervisor friend?

BUCK: A support network for people who have things they can't talk about.

KATHY: They could get together and not talk.

(BUCK *and* KATHY *sit there.*)

BUCK: Kathy. Do you want to have dinner?

KATHY: You mean, dinner?

BUCK: Well, yeah. Dinner. Why not.

KATHY: Oh Mister Sally.

BUCK: Brian.

KATHY: Brian. I've learned something, from the supervisor.

BUCK: The one who…

KATHY: Watching her, having to hide all that she's going through since they work together, it's like the tree that falls and nobody hears.

BUCK: Or being buried in ice. You're shaking and dying, but no one can know.

KATHY: I wouldn't want to become that person.

BUCK: Neither would I.

(*Without looking at* BUCK, KATHY *puts her hand on his cheek. He watches the hand.*)

7. ELIZABETH AND MATT

(ELIZABETH *reads from* MATT's *workbook.*)

ELIZABETH: Good. Yes. Yes. You broke it into parts. You solved each part for X. You added up the quotients. You nailed the answer.

MATT: All right.

ELIZABETH: How come it took you so long to ask me for help.

(MATT *doesn't answer.*)

ELIZABETH: That's what I come to your school for, right? After-school homework-helper? Why'd you never ask 'til now?

MATT: Before, life sorta sucked, so I thought, why bother. But lately, life's really sucked, so I thought, why not go for it.

ELIZABETH: Parent problems?

(MATT *looks down.*)

ELIZABETH: Old people are such hypocrites.

(MATT *nods.*)

ELIZABETH: In high school you can see the light at the end of the tunnel.

MATT: Must be great.

ELIZABETH: Anything else I can help you with?

MATT: How do you know if somebody likes you.

ELIZABETH: Oh. Well does she notice you?

(MATT *shrugs, nods.*)

ELIZABETH: When she talks to you is she excited?

MATT: I guess.

ELIZABETH: Does she, I don't know, praise you at all?

(MATT *nods.*)

ELIZABETH: Maybe she likes you.

MATT: How do I know if she wants to make out.

ELIZABETH: Put your arm around her shoulder and just leave it there. If she doesn't move away it's probably okay.

MATT: Okay.

ELIZABETH: Or sometimes you can just look into the person's eyes and bring your head closer and if they don't look away you can keep coming closer 'til it just happens.

MATT: And the thing, with your tongue…

ELIZABETH: Move it around like you're licking. But gentle.

MATT: How do you know when to start breathing hard?

ELIZABETH: That just happens.

MATT: Because of the effort of the licking?

ELIZABETH: Because you're pressing your bodies together.

MATT: Hugging.

ELIZABETH: More like slow dancing. But with your eyes closed. Then the breathing fast just happens.

MATT: Doesn't seem bad.

ELIZABETH: It's not, with somebody you like.

MATT: That's the thing.

ELIZABETH: I'm with this great guy.

(MATT *gestures awkwardly, groping for a question.*)

ELIZABETH: You'd like him. He's so cool.

MATT: He go to your school?

ELIZABETH: He was there, now he's not. It's a long story.

(MATT *nods.*)

ELIZABETH: He's really spontaneous. He just does stuff. Like he wasn't that into me at first I guess, but then he just showed up and got totally back in the picture, and now he's talking like we should go away somewhere.

MATT: You mean, leave?

ELIZABETH: I've got to get out. You know?

(MATT *nods.*)

ELIZABETH: It's so stupid here. Everybody's such a hypocrite.

MATT: Yeah.

ELIZABETH: Wouldn't that be cool? To just get on a plane and get out.

(ELIZABETH *throws her arm over* MATT'*s shoulder. He pants.*)

8. BUCK AND ELIZABETH

(BUCK *stands facing out.* ELIZABETH *paces, limping.*)

BUCK: To get to the after-school program from this floor, do I go up or down?

ELIZABETH: The gym is down and the classrooms are up.

BUCK: I pick up my son here all the time but today I got off on the wrong floor because I'm a little dizzy and my insides are falling apart.

ELIZABETH: This guy who was supposed to pick me up didn't show so I came down to use the phone but instead I kicked the wall and now maybe I'll go back up to talk to this kid who at least treats me like a human.

BUCK: Here's the elevator— *(He steps forward, starts to collapse.)* It's nothing, my body's falling apart, it does that, whenever someone puts her hand on my cheek and says yes she'll have dinner with me and then half an hour later says she just got a call from this other guy and they seem to be getting back together which I have to assume is code for she suddenly realized I'm a decrepit failure and everything I'll ever do stinks.

(BUCK collapses, ELIZABETH helps him to his feet, she starts to sink on her sore foot, he helps her up, he starts to collapse again, she helps him up.)

BUCK: It must be something to be young and beautiful.

ELIZABETH: I'm beautiful?

BUCK: Oh yes. God yes. I mean yes. Yes.

(ELIZABETH paces around, shakes out her foot.)

BUCK: Say, since you're going up you can meet my son.

ELIZABETH: Actually, I guess I'll stay here and call this guy.

BUCK: Sure. Good.

(BUCK and ELIZABETH shake hands. As they do he swoons, she steadies him.)

BUCK: Thanks.

9. KATHY AND MATT

(MATT stands there facing out. KATHY approaches.)

KATHY: I'm trying to get into the apartment complex five fifty three, do you live there?

(Pause)

(MATT *nods, without looking at* KATHY.)

KATHY: The front entrance is blocked, it says there's a path around back but I couldn't find it, I went all the way around the block twice, could you show me?

MATT: *(Thinks, looks)* I don't want to go there.

KATHY: You know what? Neither do I. Someone stands me up for dinner so I dig up his home address? Why. I'm not wanted. Forget it. And you know what else? I'm not going to run and dig up the number of this older guy whose feelings I've already hurt. No. I'm going home. Thank you.

(KATHY *starts off, comes back.*)

KATHY: Why don't *you* want to go there.

MATT: Cause. It's messed up.

KATHY: Family, huh.

(MATT *stares out.*)

KATHY: So maybe they are messed up. What're you going to do, abandon ship?

(MATT *stares out.*)

KATHY: There's no point in going off on some desperate quest that'll leave you ashamed and beaten up and disgusted when you can get all that at home. So what do you say we march home and face up to the lunatics we live with.

(MATT *nods.*)

KATHY: I'm Kathy. Who are you.

(MATT *doesn't answer.*)

KATHY: It's not like I'm going to call your parents, first name only.

MATT: Matt.

KATHY: Matt. Thank you for listening to me, Matt.

MATT: Okay. Kathy.

(KATHY hugs MATT hard, goes. He pants.)

10. TODD AND BUCK

(TODD listens to headphones and rocks back and forth. BUCK observes.)

BUCK: *(Shouts)* How about congress, huh?, I mean what are they thinking?

(TODD keeps rocking.)

BUCK: *(Shouts)* Say you've got to close the freezer all the way because the meat starts to go and there's popsicle goo on the ice cubes, so can you do that?

(TODD keeps rocking.)

BUCK: *(Shouts)* So should I get you somebody to talk to?

(TODD keeps rocking.)

BUCK: *(Shouts)* When I dropped by the office that wasn't to check up on you, I was making my quarterly visit early, I do that sometimes, all right?

(TODD keeps rocking.)

BUCK: *(Shouts)* So are you liking the people there, there are some very fine people don't you think?

(TODD keeps rocking.)

BUCK: *(Shouts)* When my dad was dying I sat up with him every night and right near the end I told him I loved him, can I tell you what the bastard said to me? can I tell you?

(TODD's rocking slows down, then speeds up.)

BUCK: *(Shouts)* So listen if you're going to leave your underwear in the hall we're trying to keep it in a pile by the stairs so I don't have to keep finding laundry all over the carpet if that's okay so all right then?

(TODD *keeps rocking.*)

BUCK: *(Longer pause, not shouting)* I'm not going to be getting a call about you in the middle of the night, am I?

(TODD *slows down, keeps rocking.*)

11. KATHY AND ELIZABETH

(ELIZABETH *and* KATHY *eat pasta.*)

KATHY: I still can't believe you're sharing the last of your sauce with me. Is it poisoned?

ELIZABETH: If you don't want it don't eat it.

KATHY: Sorry. I'm tired.

ELIZABETH: How's Sue and that guy.

KATHY: He was too young. You need a similar amount of life experience, you know?

ELIZABETH: You can make it work, if you stick with it and learn the person's language.

KATHY: You can't learn the person's language if you don't have a basis for what things mean.

ELIZABETH: You can pick up the person's logic if there's a strong feeling there, and patience.

KATHY: Patience has nothing to do with it if there's no foundation.

ELIZABETH: With attraction you can build a foundation.

KATHY: Lizzy. Listen. I've seen it up close.

ELIZABETH: I've seen it up close too, with Jenna. They had their troubles but they rode it out, they're about to go away together.

KATHY: If he's as much older than her as you said it can't last.

ELIZABETH: When the guy's the one who's older it's no problem.

KATHY: Yes it's a problem, it's disgusting.

ELIZABETH: How can you say that? They're doing great.

KATHY: Really.

ELIZABETH: There's a real bond. They're in touch. Their spirits are united.

KATHY: Their "spirits" are "united"?

ELIZABETH: They give off this glow, it's uplifting, just thinking about them makes me feel great, to see the haze from the moon on the walls, to see you eating my pasta, to—

KATHY: Your pasta?

ELIZABETH: I made the sauce, I bought the ingredients.

KATHY: With your allowance. That I gave you. Every penny. Ever think about that?

(ELIZABETH *stammers.*)

KATHY: And this sauce you call yours uses the exact same ingredients as mine, doesn't it.

ELIZABETH: No Mom.

KATHY: It uses all the same ingredients.

ELIZABETH: No Mom, mine has thyme.

KATHY: Your sauce has thyme, does it.

ELIZABETH: You heard me.

KATHY: But who exposed you to thyme in the first place, huh? Who gave you your first taste of every combination that's ever entered your mouth? And where do you think you got the ability to intuit what's appropriate to begin with? The courage to trust your own hunches? You think that comes in a vacuum? The sense that contrast is fine? That heat can be good? The feeling of food going down? Not to be frightened of that? Or that there's pleasure in warmth? The way you experience moisture? You got all that from me before you could talk or even reach, before you had eyes, you absorbed that through my skin and my pulse so don't sit there and tell me it's your pasta.

12. ELIZABETH AND TODD

(ELIZABETH *and Todd stand there.*)

ELIZABETH: You did say meet you at the bus. You didn't say meet by a tree seven blocks from the bus.

TODD: I left you a note.

ELIZABETH: Where.

TODD: Behind a sign.

ELIZABETH: What sign.

TODD: A stop sign.

ELIZABETH: Why did you do that?

TODD: There was a spider. And a man with one eye. He stopped, and stepped over the spider, non-stop.

(ELIZABETH *and* TODD *stand there.*)

ELIZABETH: Should we take a taxi to the airport?

TODD: You have to be open to new ways of arriving.

ELIZABETH: I'm open to any way of arriving, just so we get there soon.

TODD: Let's be quiet now.

ELIZABETH: Todd. I've heard how after people do what we did things can get weird, people act different, and people expect different things. But this is new to me.

You've got to clue me in on what to say now or we're going to miss our plane to Hawaii.

TODD: I'm in the breeze. I'm touching down. My legs are there but my head isn't. It's a stretch.

ELIZABETH: Are you on drugs?

TODD: I'm too old to be this young. I'm too young to be this old.

ELIZABETH: Maybe we should get to know each other better before we go to Hawaii.

TODD: I need to ask you something.

ELIZABETH: Okay.

TODD: Are you in Hawaii?

ELIZABETH: No.

TODD: Am I in Hawaii?

ELIZABETH: No.

TODD: I'm really not in Hawaii.

ELIZABETH: No.

TODD: Oh.

ELIZABETH: So what do you want to do.

TODD: I want to plunge to my death.

13. KATHY AND TODD

(TODD *sits, not quite conscious.* KATHY *sits beside him.*)

KATHY: Birds could knock over trains. I read that somewhere. If they were human size. Their wings are fifty times stronger than our arms. So they can leap out of trees and fly away. But we have to stay on the ground and talk things out. I'm so glad you had them call me. But I need to tell you something. The medicine they've given you is going to wear off, and they can't keep you here. They're scared you'll jump again. And I'm scared. So you need to give them the name of a family member. A family member could take custody. You have a problem and you need to be looked after. Can you hear me? There was another visitor before me but they said she wasn't related to you, right? Listen. I've decided. I want to meet the people in your life. And I want you to meet the people in my life. I want us all to get together. I dream of that. I don't even care, where it leads, or if you like her more than me. I like other people too. I just want all of us talking. That would begin the healing, I believe, for you, and for us all. Everyone opening up their mouths in one great big conversation. But that can't even begin to happen, unless you speak up.

14. BUCK AND MATT

(MATT *lies on his belly staring into his magazine. Buck stands, holding his book, watching Matt.*)

MATT: You got something to tell me.

(BUCK *doesn't answer.*)

MATT: It's about Todd. Right?

(BUCK *doesn't answer.*)

MATT: If you can't say it maybe write it down.

(BUCK *struggles to write in his book, his hand shaking wildly.*)

15. ELIZABETH AND KATHY

(ELIZABETH *sits on a pillow with her notebook, not writing.*
KATHY *sits in a chair reading, making markings in her*
book.)

ELIZABETH: I need to ask you a question.

KATHY: What.

ELIZABETH: Why is it sometimes you have the idea for
what you're going to write but when you sit down to
write it's totally gone.

KATHY: It'll come, it always does.

ELIZABETH: And how come sometimes you start
working on something and it goes to this other place
you didn't expect it to go and you're not even sure that
you like it.

KATHY: It's funny how that happens isn't it.

ELIZABETH: And how come people leave us, Mom. We
meet someone and it's going so great but then all of a
sudden it goes wrong. And you don't even know what
you did. You didn't even do anything. And how come
people start treating us badly? Why do they do that,
Mom? And sometimes people die, why is that. And
things end. You're with someone and it ends. You get
married and you do all this stuff to make it good but it
ends. Every relationship ends somehow Mom. Every
single time you get together with somebody that ends.
The person starts treating you badly or changes or
else the person dies. Or else you die. How do we keep
starting up again and again Mom. How do we keep
getting dressed and doing things and talking to people
and falling in love with people over and over again?
How do we do that.

KATHY: I don't know, my darling. But we do.

(ELIZABETH *and* KATHY *hug.)*

16. KATHY, ELIZABETH, BUCK, MATT, TODD

(KATHY *sits, makes markings in her big book.* ELIZABETH *sits on a pillow, writes in her notebook.* BUCK *sits, working with his very big book.* MATT *lies on his belly, reading his magazine. Todd sits in the center, typing.*)

(ELIZABETH *taps her foot.*)

KATHY: *(Not looking)* Shh.

(ELIZABETH *looks at* KATHY, *who isn't looking at her, then looks over to* TODD. TODD *and* ELIZABETH *have a private moment—a shared look and/or touch unseen by the others, then go back to their work.*)

(TODD *and* KATHY *have a private moment, then go back to their work.*)

(KATHY *and* MATT *have a private moment, then go back to their work.*)

(ELIZABETH *and* MATT *have a private moment, then go back to their work.*)

(BUCK *and* ELIZABETH *have a private moment, then go back to their work.*)

(KATHY *and* BUCK *have a private moment, then go back to their work.*)

(*All five lean together, so that each is touching someone else, while still focused on their work.*)

(*All look out, then go back to their work.*)

END OF PLAY

BEATLES FOREVER

CHARACTERS

PAUL
LAURA
JOHN
MYRA
GEORGE
SYDNEY
RINGO
ANNE MARIE

(A hotel room. The Beatles as in their famous 1964 performances—dark jackets, white shirts, ties, with "mop top" haircuts—getting comfortable with four American female fans: PAUL *with* LAURA, JOHN *with* MYRA, GEORGE *with* SYDNEY, RINGO *with* ANNE MARIE. *The women are also dressed in early sixties fashion, and wear their hair in the styles of the day.)*

LAURA: I can't believe you really are who you are.

PAUL: I think I'm who I am.

JOHN: I'm not. I'm who he is. *(Refers to* GEORGE*)*

GEORGE: I thought *I* was who I am.

RINGO: *(To* JOHN*)* You can't both be who he is.

GEORGE: I'd rather be who you are. *(Refers to* RINGO*)*

PAUL: *I* want to be him. *(Refers to* RINGO*)*

RINGO: *(To* PAUL*)* I don't think I'd like you as me.

JOHN: *(To* PAUL*)* So you'll just have to be who you are.

PAUL: And who's that?

GEORGE, JOHN: Me.

(The Beatles laugh, the women scream.)

MYRA: *(To* LAURA*)* I know what you mean, it's unbelievable.

LAURA: They were on that stage a few minutes ago.

MYRA: It's really them.

SYDNEY: We're really with them.

LAURA: They chose us from the whole screaming crowd and now we're—

(ANNE MARIE *giggles uncontrollably, grabs* RINGO.)

PAUL: *(To* RINGO*)* She loves you.

JOHN: Yeah.

GEORGE: Yeah.

RINGO: Yeah.

(All couples begin making out. As they do, they move around, strolling, tumbling, rolling. All move offstage or upstage behind couches and are hidden, except for LAURA *and* PAUL, *who drift downstage. She, suddenly troubled, breaks away from him.)*

LAURA: It's a dream. You. With me. I'm dreaming.

PAUL: If it's a dream, it's a lovely dream, right?

LAURA: It's so incredible it makes me scared and sad.

PAUL: Why would a lovely dream scare you and make you sad?

LAURA: I don't know.

PAUL: It's a dream for me too you know.

LAURA: It is?

PAUL: It's a really lovely dream for me because you're really lovely.

LAURA: You? Saying that about me? I'm dreaming. I'm dreaming.

PAUL: Look, Laura. Most dreams aren't lovely at all. They're scary and lonely and awful. So let's just love this lovely dream for as long as we're dreaming it.

*(*LAURA *and* PAUL *resume making out, drift off.* JOHN *and* MYRA *drift down. She breaks away from him.)*

MYRA: What's it like being you?

JOHN: Mustard. Cellophane. Walrus. What's it like being you?

MYRA: Strawberry.

JOHN: We have a lot in common.

MYRA: How do you do it?

JOHN: It being what?

MYRA: You say exactly what everyone's thinking and feeling before anyone has any idea they're thinking and feeling it.

JOHN: Well I just googoogajoob.

MYRA: No one does what you do.

JOHN: You should introduce me to no one. If he does what I do we should team up.

MYRA: Why do you pick apart everything I say?

JOHN: Because these words coming from you are my only clue y'know, the only thing I have that's come from inside your head. I pick your words apart, shake them around, squeeze them to see what's inside, so I can see what's inside you.

MYRA: So what's inside me?

JOHN: Yes.

MYRA: Yes.

(JOHN *and* MYRA *resume making out, go upstage,* GEORGE *and* SYDNEY *come down. She breaks away from him.*)

SYDNEY: This isn't me.

GEORGE: In what sense?

SYDNEY: I'm not who I really am yet. Who I need to be, and will be. Not nearly.

GEORGE: You think this is who I really am?

SYDNEY: I see more of you than you realize.

GEORGE: I see more of you than you realize.

SYDNEY: What do you see of me?

GEORGE: Something from the way you move.

SYDNEY: What.

(GEORGE *sings a whining guitar sound, the first four notes of the guitar solo in* Something.)

SYDNEY: It makes me feel all this…

GEORGE: What.

SYDNEY: Something.

GEORGE: What do you see of me?

SYDNEY: I don't have any way to say it, except…

(SYDNEY *kisses* GEORGE, *they resume making out, go upstage.* ANNE MARIE *and* RINGO *come downstage. She is giggling. He tries to kiss her.*)

ANNE MARIE: I'm about to be kissed by Ringo. Ringo. Ringo.

RINGO: Could you try to forget I'm Ringo for a minute so I can kiss you?

ANNE MARIE: How could I forget you're Ringo? You're so Ringo.

RINGO: How about if you try just thinking I'm Ringo?

ANNE MARIE: I shouldn't say you're Ringo? I'll try, Ringo. I'd do anything for you, Ringo.

RINGO: This is really frustrating.

ANNE MARIE: Oh Ringo, when you sit at the drums, shaking your head, I can't help screaming. Do you want to hear me scream, Ringo?

RINGO: (*Shakes his head*) No.

(ANNE MARIE *screams.*)

RINGO: (*Shakes his head*) Please don't.

ANNE MARIE: I have to scream when you shake your head Ringo, is that all right?

RINGO: *(Shakes his head)* No.

(ANNE MARIE screams, sobs.)

RINGO: You all right there?

ANNE MARIE: After tonight we'll never see each other again.

RINGO: How can you know what'll happen in the future?

ANNE MARIE: You mean, we might see more of each other?

RINGO: Anything's possible in America.

ANNE MARIE: Oh Ringo. Ringo.

(ANNE MARIE assaults RINGO with kisses. They drift off upstage. LAURA comes downstage, calls the other women.)

LAURA: Psst!

(ANNE MARIE, MYRA, and SYDNEY join LAURA downstage.)

ANNE MARIE: What.

MYRA: What is it.

SYDNEY: What.

LAURA: I want us to mean something to them.

ANNE MARIE: Us, mean something to them?

SYDNEY: What could we mean to them, really?

MYRA: They're who they are.

ANNE MARIE: And we're who we are.

LAURA: But with them meaning so much, and us meaning so little, it's feels scary, like they could replace us any second.

MYRA: I actually wondered if they might be losing interest, just a bit.

ANNE MARIE: I wondered that too.

SYDNEY: Really?

MYRA: At first they were really excited, really quick to say nice things.

LAURA: They were.

MYRA: Now they're, I don't know

ANNE MARIE: Not so quick.

(They think.)

SYDNEY: What if we changed something about ourselves. Just a little something, about how we look. So they see us like for the first time.

MYRA: Okay.

ANNE MARIE: Yeah.

LAURA: Let's do it.

(The four women put on a little makeup, adjust their hair slightly, straighten their clothes. They go back upstage, to find:)

(The Beatles are transformed. They wear brightly-colored baggy clothes, love beads, one wears granny glasses, another wears epaulets, another wears an animal mask, another wears a wizard cap. They have an assortment of beards, moustaches, long hair.)

LAURA: Who are you?

PAUL: We're who we always were.

GEORGE: Who we really were.

JOHN: Who we were before wasn't who we really are at all.

RINGO: *(To* JOHN*)* I'm always who I really am.

JOHN: *(To* RINGO*)* You're full of yourself.

PAUL: We're all full of ourselves now.

GEORGE: Our selves are full of us.

PAUL: *(To the women)* And we're still all yours.

LAURA: Is this a joke?

MYRA: I don't get it.

ANNE MARIE: You look like a circus from the eighteen nineties.

SYDNEY: Where'd get you this stuff?

MYRA: And why.

LAURA: What you were thinking?

PAUL: We weren't thinking really.

JOHN: Well, we were thinking but

PAUL: As you get started something happens.

GEORGE: It comes from inside.

RINGO: It just does.

PAUL: You're doing it, actually, but

JOHN: It feels like it's doing you.

GEORGE: And before you know it things are coming out of you that you didn't know were possible.

PAUL: And there you are.

ANNE MARIE: Are you on something?

JOHN: I don't think we're on anything.

PAUL: If we were on something we'd be the first to know.

RINGO: Once I was on something so strong I didn't even know I was on it.

GEORGE: Then how do you know you were on it?

RINGO: *(Beat)* I don't know.

(The Beatles laugh.)

ANNE MARIE, LAURA, MYRA, SYDNEY: *(Ad lib, all speaking at the same time, to each other)* It's so weird, right? This is all so weird. They're being weird. So weird. It's just weird is what it is it really is, it really is so weird.

(The Beatles approach the women and start tickling them.)

GEORGE, JOHN, PAUL, RINGO: *(Ad lib, all speaking at the same time, to the women)* Come on, take it easy. Come on, this is who we are. Come on, enjoy who we are. Come on, this is still us, we're just being what we really are.

(LAURA breaks away. She gasps.)

MYRA & SYDNEY: What.

ANNE MARIE: What.

LAURA: The change in who they are is making me feel, different.

SYDNEY: Me too.

LAURA: *(Walking all around)* More free.

SYDNEY: I know what you—

ANNE MARIE: Yeah yeah yeah there's this feeling like anything is okay you can be anything do anything. *(Gasps and gasps and gasps)*

MYRA: I don't know. I don't get it.

JOHN: This is mustard cellophane walrus.

MYRA: No it's not.

JOHN: Maybe it's not your mustard cellophane walrus but it's mine. I'm sorry it's not strawberry enough for you.

MYRA: What I see is you trying to be you.

JOHN: *(Shouts)* I'm not trying to be anything. Can't you see that? What I was before wasn't me, and soon I'll see that this wasn't me. I'm in between two things, always, that's who I am. I've never been some *one*. I don't even know what I'm saying, can't you see that?

MYRA: Why are you shouting?

JOHN: Because I can't get my words through your head. *(He storms off.)*

MYRA: John. *(She follows JOHN off.)*

LAURA: *(Still walking all around)* I don't feel this need to keep a certain distance from people or stand a certain way because somebody's looking, I don't need to say something just because we made eye contact, I can say what I want how I want and just keep moving.

SYDNEY: *(Stands very still)* I don't need to move at all, I can let my arms hang down. *(Her arms drift)* Or drift.

ANNE MARIE: *(Taking off her shoes, loosening her clothes)* Why am I wearing shoes? What am I hiding? I have feet. And legs. And thighs.

LAURA: *(Swirling)* To just be myself feels so good. *(Sighs)*

SYDNEY: *(Moving her arms)* I am who I am. Finally. *(Hums)*

ANNE MARIE: *(Loosening her clothes, discovering her body)* I'm me. I'm me. *(Pants)*

PAUL: It looks like they're on something.

GEORGE: They're on us.

RINGO: I wish they'd be on us by being on us.

(The sounds ANNE MARIE, LAURA, and SYDNEY are making intensify until:)

(MYRA, off, screams.)

PAUL: What?

LAURA: What?

(MYRA *comes out.*)

RINGO: What is it?

MYRA: He's, he's…

(*We hear* JOHN *over speakers, but don't see him.*)

JOHN: *(Invisible)* I'm not here.

ANNE MARIE: What?

MYRA: He's not here.

SYDNEY: But I hear you.

JOHN: *(Invisible)* You hear me because I'm not here.

LAURA: I don't understand.

JOHN: *(Invisible)* I don't stand anywhere. I'm nowhere. Nothing. Nobody.

ANNE MARIE: Whoa.

LAURA: *(To* PAUL*)* You're doing this, right? Like when you changed before? It's a trick or something?

GEORGE: It's not something, it's nothing.

RINGO: Nothing is real.

PAUL: We have nothing to do with nowhere.

RINGO: Nobody does.

LAURA: *(To* PAUL*)* Then how did—

JOHN: *(Invisible)* It just happened. It didn't make any sense.

ANNE MARIE: You, uh

JOHN: *(Invisible)* Just when I was starting to think I knew who I was and who I wasn't I stopped being anybody at all.

MYRA: *(Wringing her hands, sinking)* My bones feel heavy. I'm trying to think about good things but I keep thinking about bad things. Shit. I'm old. Your not being here has made me not what I was.

LAURA/ANNE MARIE/SYDNEY: *(Wringing their hands, sinking)* Yeah. / Shit. / God.

JOHN: *(Invisible)* I don't miss changing people. I miss holding people and kissing them.

(GEORGE starts to go.)

SYDNEY: *(To GEORGE)* Where are you going?

(GEORGE slips away, disappears. His voice comes from speakers.)

GEORGE: *(Invisible)* Nowhere.

SYDNEY: Why did you do that?

GEORGE: *(Invisible)* I didn't do anything. It was happening so I went with the flow.

MYRA: Are you with John?

GEORGE: *(Invisible)* I'm not nowhere with anybody. I'm not even with myself.

(LAURA screams softly.)

ANNE MARIE: Okay. Everybody out. Come on.

JOHN: *(Invisible)* I don't know how to come out of nothing.

GEORGE: *(Invisible)* I don't know how I got into nothing.

PAUL: *(To RINGO)* What do you see when you're in the dark?

RINGO: *(To PAUL)* Nothing. But at least it's mine.

MYRA: I don't get this.

JOHN: *(Invisible)* You can't get it, you have to imagine it.

SYDNEY: I'm trying to imagine it. I can't.

GEORGE: *(Invisible)* Just because you can't imagine something doesn't mean it can't be. Nearly everything that is, is unimaginable, but it still is.

LAURA: What are you saying?

JOHN: *(Invisible)* We're not saying anything.

GEORGE: *(Invisible)* When you hear us, that's just you hearing things. It's not us saying things.

MYRA: In other words

LAURA: Are you us?

MYRA: Are we nobody?

GEORGE: *(Invisible, makes the whining guitar sound)*

SYDNEY: Ow. It hurts.

LAURA: What hurts?

ANNE MARIE: How?

SYDNEY: I don't know. Something.

GEORGE: *(Invisible)* I'm without you from within.

JOHN: *(Invisible)* I'm a no I mean a yes.

(SYDNEY screams softly.)

(MYRA screams softly.)

PAUL: *(Low groan)* Uhhhhhhhhh…

JOHN: *(Invisible, low groan)* Uhhhhhhhhh…

GEORGE: *(Invisible, low groan)* Uhhhhhhhhhh….

RINGO: *(Low groan)* Uhhhhhhhhhh…

(Their low groans go up in pitch, swirling higher and higher, louder and louder, the women run around screaming in horror, pull their hair, their clothes, until—)

LAURA: PSST!

(The women come together downstage. PAUL and RINGO drift off into darkness.)

LAURA: They're dragging us around by our guts and our brains.

MYRA: My whole feeling of me, they grab it and twist it.

ANNE MARIE: They're these weird magicians.

LAURA: Or ghosts.

MYRA: They're playing with us.

LAURA: I'm scared to go back to them, I have no idea what they'll be.

ANNE MARIE: I'm not going back to them.

SYDNEY: We don't have a choice.

MYRA: Of course we have a choice, we can always just go home.

ANNE MARIE: It's late. My parents are sitting up with their newspapers, their bedroom slippers, their Lawrence Welk. I should go.

SYDNEY: We can't go.

MYRA: What do you mean?

SYDNEY: There are some places, once you've been there, you're always there.

LAURA: *(Shouts)* That makes no sense. I'm going.

ANNE MARIE: Me too.

MYRA: Me too.

(As ANNE MARIE, LAURA, *and* MYRA *start off, they come face to face with* GEORGE, JOHN, PAUL, *and* RINGO, *all dressed as at first, in '64-style suits and haircuts. The Beatles stand there silently.)*

MYRA: *(To* JOHN*)* Is it you?

SYDNEY: George?

LAURA: *(To* PAUL*)* So you're back to what you were?

ANNE MARIE: *(To* RINGO*)* Hello? Hello?

MYRA: *(To* JOHN*)* Are you there?

JOHN: I think I'm here.

PAUL: *(To* JOHN*)* It looks like you're there.

GEORGE: He might be there but not be him.

RINGO: Who else would he be?

GEORGE: Nobody.

PAUL: I thought he was nobody.

JOHN: I got over it.

RINGO: *(To* GEORGE*)* You were nobody too.

SYDNEY: *(To* GEORGE*)* I missed you.

GEORGE: I missed me too.

MYRA: *(To* JOHN*)* So what happened?

LAURA: *(To* PAUL*)* Are you going to stay like this?

ANNE MARIE: *(To* RINGO*)* Are you ever going to be nobody?

SYDNEY: *(To* GEORGE*)* Are you really here? Really?

PAUL: You Americans have got to stop trying to understand everything.

RINGO: We don't really know how we got to be what we are or what we'll be the next time we turn around.

GEORGE: We don't know how somebody becomes somebody and then somebody else and then nobody and then somebody again.

JOHN: We don't know why when some people become nobody you still hear them but when somebody else becomes nobody no one even notices that they've gone.

PAUL: But whatever we are and whatever you are we know that in one way or another we're here and you're here.

JOHN: We're all together.

RINGO: So let's hold each other and kiss and love each other because

JOHN: love is what you'll always have whatever happens.

GEORGE: Love is what you leave behind wherever you go.

PAUL: All the things we say and sing to each other only matter because of what they make people feel.

RINGO: It's not who you are, it's, y'know, are you holding someone's hand.

JOHN: —that makes this whole unreal whatever-it-is feel like it's real.

GEORGE: Everything is incredibly complex and weird but it's also simple, really.

(Pause. The women take a moment. The Beatles wait. Suddenly—)

LAURA: *(Has an insight, weeps)* All you need is love.

(LAURA embraces PAUL.)

MYRA: *(Has an insight, squeals)* Love *is* all you need.

(MYRA embraces JOHN.)

SYDNEY: *(Has an insight, trembles)* Love is *all*.

(SYDNEY embraces GEORGE.)

ANNE MARIE: *(Has an insight, shrugs)* Love is all.

(ANNE MARIE embraces RINGO.)

(The women and Beatles begin to make love.)

PAUL: Yeah.

JOHN: Yeah.

GEORGE: Yeah.

(ANNE MARIE giggles.)

RINGO: Yeah.

(All make love. Slow fade)

END OF PLAY

AT THE BEACH

CHARACTERS

ADINA
SARAH
ERIC
JOE

(ADINA *and* SARAH, *wearing bathing suits and sunglasses, sit on beach chairs.*)

ADINA: I let you speak so you need to let me speak.

SARAH: You didn't let me speak.

ADINA: I did. I let you make your point. I sat here and I listened.

SARAH: You didn't let me finish.

ADINA: I didn't listen to you? I didn't sit here?

SARAH: But when I reminded you that in the kitchen—

ADINA: You said that, now it's my turn.

SARAH: You stood in the kitchen—

ADINA: I let you make your point so now let me finish. Let me finish.

SARAH: You stood there—

ADINA: I couldn't have stood there and told you I was choosing the beach because it was *your* turn to choose where we go for vacation so for Labor Day we're seeing *my* parents.

SARAH: But *I* didn't choose the beach, *you* did.

ADINA: You mentioned a few places and I said I thought the beach would be the least problematic but it was your choice to ask for my input in the first place and your choice to go along with my suggestion and so we're visiting *my* parents for Labor Day because that's how we do it.

SARAH: I know that's how we do it and that's why I let *you* choose where we'd go for summer vacation so we could see *my* parents over Labor Day.

ADINA: You've got to stop saying that okay because it doesn't get us anywhere and we need to get somewhere with this so please stop bringing up the kitchen because it was nothing, you mentioned some things, I said some things, I wasn't even sitting down— All year we plan our summer trip and everybody plans around our plans so it's ridiculous to let one little conversation—should I be afraid to go into the kitchen in the morning?, is that the message?, that I should avoid the kitchen when you're having breakfast so you don't get me into some tricky questionnaire that you'll throw back in my face?

SARAH: I asked in plain English—

ADINA: I hate the beach, all right, so this is hard enough, to enjoy *your* vacation that *you* chose, and the only thing that makes it endurable is knowing that we're going to visit *my* parents, who think you hate them, because we never see them.

SARAH: We saw them last month.

ADINA: You're counting a funeral?

SARAH: We could see them at Christmas.

ADINA: How could I tell them to wait until Christmas? How could I possibly justify—

SARAH: My parents are taking our son this week.

ADINA: Yes. And so. And so.

SARAH: They're taking our son so we can have a vacation.

ADINA: I think I know that.

SARAH: They're always the ones who take our son.

ADINA: Yes. And they love taking our son.

SARAH: So we owe them the visit.

ADINA: You're saying after giving your parents all that time with our son we should give them more time with us all instead of staying with my parents who are expecting us?, that's like saying I gave you money so now I have to cook you dinner—but look, look. What matters is, this is a beach. It's your perfect place.

SARAH: No it's not.

ADINA: This isn't a beach?

SARAH: It's not the beach I would have chosen.

ADINA: Who else would choose a beach. Me? Would I choose a beach? You actually believe I would choose a beach?

SARAH: Yes.

ADINA: You honestly believe I would choose, out of all the—

SARAH: Yes.

ADINA: I would choose a beach.

SARAH: Yes.

ADINA: I. Me.

SARAH: You did once.

ADINA: I chose a beach.

SARAH: Yes.

ADINA: I chose a beach. I chose a beach.

SARAH: Yes.

ADINA: Look. We can't just make things up. That's so important here.

SARAH: That first summer, you chose a beach.

ADINA: We'd just met. Of course I chose a beach when we'd just met. Who wouldn't choose a beach when they'd just met. You loved the beach. So I said fine, the beach, the beach. But that was twenty plus years ago, I'm not a beach person, you know that, but hey look don't feel bad, that's not what this is about, I appreciate your asking for input, that was very considerate, and I don't hate the beach, I enjoy being on the sand, watching the waves, this is fine, I love your choice, so let's enjoy, we'll enjoy it, and we'll see your parents briefly when we pick up the boy, then on Labor Day we'll call them from my parents'.

SARAH: They're counting on us this Labor Day because they're old and they're scared.

ADINA: Scared are they?, my dad's collapsed twice, my mom can't remember where she leaves the car, just because my parents don't have conditions with Latin names doesn't mean they don't need to see us—yes your parents are scared, they've been scared, they'll keep on being scared, so let's see them at Christmas, everybody's scared at Christmas, just imagine how scared they'll be then.

SARAH: My mother said if we—

ADINA: No no no no she can't manipulate us.

SARAH: She said—

ADINA: We can't let that woman run our lives.

SARAH: *(Grabs* ADINA's *arm)* Listen.

ADINA: You're shoving me?

SARAH: She said that if—

ADINA: You can't make your point with words so you're going to start shoving? Is that how you want it?

SARAH: I was getting your attention.

ADINA: To get attention we should start shoving?

SARAH: She said that—

ADINA: Would you like it if I got your attention that way? Would you like that? Is that what you want? I should start shoving? I should shove?

(SARAH *slumps over as if asleep.*)

ADINA: You can't do that. You can't just drop out. It's cruel and destructive and unfair. So you're getting points now, is that it? You're winning something? *(She springs up, paces around snapping her fingers, storms off to the left.)*

(ERIC, *wearing bathing trunks, enters from the right, slows down, comes to a stop, clenches his fists and has a spasm of trembling, stands there.*)

(JOE, *wearing bathing trunks, enters from the left.*)

JOE: Eric. Hey.

ERIC: Joe. How's it going?

JOE: I'm good. How are you.

ERIC: Okay.

JOE: How long are you down for?

ERIC: Just the weekend. How 'bout you?

JOE: The whole month. I rented a place.

ERIC: How's philosophy.

JOE: I put that aside, got into real estate. It went great so I retired. Now I write poetry. You were in law school.

ERIC: I'm at a small firm. I do free speech.

JOE: I heard you married Kessler's daughter.

ERIC: It just ended.

JOE: I'm sorry.

ERIC: My second divorce.

JOE: Women.

ERIC: How 'bout you?

JOE: Since Allie I've had three really good relationships.

ERIC: I still feel bad about Allie.

JOE: She was nuts, please.

ERIC: You two were basically through by then, right?

JOE: She was insane, really.

ERIC: But out of respect for you, I shouldn't have—

JOE: She was a maniac.

ERIC: Anyway.

(ERIC *and* JOE *stand there.*)

ERIC: You saved enough from work that you can just write poems?

JOE: Plus my parents died. I'm rich.

ERIC: It's what they would have wanted.

JOE: Writing keeps me in touch with my feelings. I'm putting together a—

(ERIC *clenches his fists and has a spasm of trembling, pause, has another spasm, gestures "one minute", catches his breath.*)

JOE: You should quit your practice and try writing.

ERIC: My parents haven't died.

JOE: You've saved enough by now, right?

ERIC: I enjoy my work.

JOE: The routine gives you comfort, but it lets you lose sight of your self.

ERIC: I'll be fine.

JOE: Kessler's daughter was half your age. Your first marriage ended in divorce, you just told me. And before that was Allie who was a complete lunatic. Maybe you should step back and take a look.

ERIC: Actually I'm with somebody now who's really great.

JOE: Really.

ERIC: *(Indicates* SARAH*)* She's sleeping. Shh.

JOE: Lovely.

ERIC: Thanks.

JOE: Really cute.

*(*ERIC *shrugs.)*

JOE: You moved right on. I'm impressed. I underestimated you, Eric.

ERIC: I'm sure you'll find somebody soon.

JOE: I'm seeing somebody now. *(Points off left)* Over there.

ERIC: Pacing and snapping her fingers?

JOE: She does that.

ERIC: Attractive woman. Very lively.

JOE: She's a sweetie.

ERIC: It used to be when you were going with somebody it was the first thing out of your mouth. You've come a long way since Allie.

JOE: So have you. Hey, since your friend is sleeping, and mine is doing her thing, why don't we head to the boardwalk and check out the Chinese Octopus.

ERIC: It's still there?

JOE: They rebuilt it.

ERIC: I can't do rides any more. I throw up.

JOE: Just to bask in the sights, the sounds, the smells.

ERIC: The Chinese octopus. Let's go.

(They start to go off to the right, SARAH sits up.)

JOE: *(To* ERIC*)* One second.

*(*JOE *goes over to* SARAH*.)*

JOE: This man is a rock. Brilliant. Incredibly successful. The handsomest guy in the tri-state area. You've noticed that of course, but you might not know that the reason he's admired far and wide is, he really cares about people. I've known Eric since third grade, and in all those years, I've never heard him say a bad word about anybody. He's always sticking up for the new kid, speaking out for the room mate everybody else thinks is a jerk, making sure nobody's left out of a bachelor party, he's the best friend you could ask for, besides being fantastic at ping pong, an awesome trombone player, and a crossword puzzle god. *(To* ERIC*)* To the Octopus?

*(*ADINA *enters.)*

ERIC: Hold on.

*(*ERIC *addresses* ADINA*.)*

ERIC: Most of us just go through life accepting things as they are. But not Joe. If your soft ball team is in a rut he's the one to get everybody charged up. If there's a party and nobody's dancing, he'll dance, and then everybody'll jump in, because he's a leader. He's the one to get everybody volunteering for a cause, visiting a guy in the hospital, checking out a new jazz club, the new food on the menu—be sure to get him to make you his pizza with ham and pineapple. He sees possibility, is the thing, a way that life can be better, and he won't rest until you see it too. *(To* JOE*)* Shall we?

ADINA: Pizza with ham and pineapple, I like that. I've never tried it but I'd like to because I like the contrast, salty and sweet. I constantly find myself having to come up with concepts, for professional reasons, and those I've done the best with as often as not—

SARAH: Shut up.

(ADINA *storms off to the left.*)

JOE: (*In the direction of* ADINA) Babe.

(SARAH *slumps over as if asleep.* ERIC *clenches his fists, has a spasm.*)

JOE: So our girlfriends didn't hit it off. That happens. But I love yours, she's wonderfully direct, and the stuff you said about me—

ERIC: What you said about me was wrong. I'm not a good person. I'm a liar. I lie.

JOE: Well, we all—

ERIC: And I'm not successful. I want to be a husband. I want to be a dad.

JOE: You will be, if you want.

ERIC: No I won't.

JOE: How can you say that?

ERIC: Because I won't. No one is ever going to call me dad.

JOE: I'm sorry, Eric.

ERIC: And I'm not a good friend. I went after Allie the minute she left you.

JOE: It happens.

ERIC: It ruined our friendship.

JOE: That was my fault too.

ERIC: I said things about you to Allie.

(JOE *stands there.*)

ERIC: When we were starting out, I used to let her say stuff about you. I didn't defend you. I even joined in.

We made fun of you behind your back. I wanted to fuck a beautiful woman so I said bad things about my friend.

JOE: You did.

ERIC: Yeah.

JOE: Well, I forgive you.

ERIC: Why?

JOE: Because, look. Sometimes that stuff matters. Who said what twenty-six years ago. Who got married. Who had kids. Who did what for money. But today, standing here, it doesn't matter.

ERIC: What does matter.

JOE: Having somebody to walk with to the Chinese Octopus.

(ERIC and JOE hug, go off to the right.)

(ADINA returns from the left, sits. SARAH sits up.)

ADINA: People find you desirable. So you can draw people in by just sitting there. But I have to open my mouth to have even a fighting chance. So it's not fair for you to humiliate me when I'm just trying to keep up with you.

SARAH: You are desirable. *(Pause)* And I don't hate your parents. *(Pause)* And if you avoid the kitchen when I'm having breakfast…I'll die.

(ADINA and SARAH sit there facing out.)

ADINA: I love you.

SARAH: I love you.

(ADINA and SARAH each reach a finger under the left eye of their sunglasses, wipe. They sit there. They sniffle in unison. They sit there.)

END OF PLAY

FREE WILL

CHARACTERS & SETTING

VIOLA
FALSTAFF
IAGO
PROSPERO
HAMLET
CLEOPATRA
JULIET
WITCH

The play takes place on an island, once upon a time.

Note: The character SEBASTIAN *appears, played by the actress who plays* VIOLA.

Another note: A couple bushes or trees on the sides of the stage indicate the edge of a forest. But the main set piece is a single, very large rock.

(A large rock. VIOLA stands there.)

VIOLA: My brother's dead and I'm alive. He was standing right next to me on the ship when the storm hit. The water took him straight down, carried me to this island. Someone's coming. Someone big. This is not a good time to be a woman. From now on, I'm not Viola.

(VIOLA hides behind the rock. FALSTAFF enters.)

FALSTAFF: You back there, are you a woman?

VIOLA: I'm Cesario.

FALSTAFF: I'm Falstaff, I was asking because the three of us on the island are all men and I need a woman to hold onto. I'm so shaken up, I was hiding in a laundry basket my friends dumped in the river when a wave came from nowhere and, are you going to come out?

VIOLA: Not yet. My clothes, got, uh—

FALSTAFF: This amazingly kind man is passing out things he's found washed up, he might have some clothes for you, here he comes now. Iago.

(IAGO enters with a bag of stuff.)

FALSTAFF: Do you have clothes for Cesario here?

IAGO: Help yourself.

(IAGO hands bag to VIOLA, who changes behind the rock.)

VIOLA: Thanks, Iago.

IAGO: You're the first one to need clothes. The storm dropped the rest of us here completely dry.

FALSTAFF: It's amazing how delicately the storm went about completely fucking up our lives.

IAGO: I'd just been promoted to captain. How many years of eating shit that took. The general chose me to accompany his wife on a ship, the waves dragged me away, it's all shot to hell. Better find us more food so we don't fucking starve.

(VIOLA *comes out dressed as a man.*)

IAGO: Here's some fruit for you.

(IAGO *hands* VIOLA *a piece of fruit, goes.*)

FALSTAFF: It's really tangy.

VIOLA: I'm not hungry. You take it.

FALSTAFF: Just finished mine. You're sure? Well, why waste. *(Bites)* It's so great to have a tongue. You put something on this one little muscle for a few seconds and all the shit in your life makes no difference. *(Finishes eating)* I'm going to go masturbate. If you want to join me…

(FALSTAFF *exits.* VIOLA *sits there.*)

VIOLA: Even when my brother and I were on different continents I knew he was somewhere.

(PROSPERO *enters carrying a staff, waves it,* VIOLA *falls asleep. He points to her, and to places where other characters have exited.*)

PROSPERO: One two three four? *(Calls)* Witch.

(PROSPERO *snaps his fingers as he exits and* VIOLA *opens her eyes.* HAMLET *enters with a knife.*)

HAMLET: I knew what had to be done, I was the only one who could do it, but I thought and I thought about doing it til they sent me away, the storm dumped me here, I'm stuck knowing it's all getting worse everyone's being lied to, abused by that shit-head.

Human beings are amazing creatures, we build towers,
fill the planet with music, but to me it's all diseased, I
can't cure it *(Screams)*

VIOLA: Stop beating yourself up.

HAMLET: Why.

VIOLA: You have a brilliant mind and a heart, big noble
goals, to get all that working together takes time.

HAMLET: I'm Hamlet.

VIOLA: Cesario.

HAMLET: We'll never get off this island, will we.

VIOLA: Focus on something else.

HAMLET: What.

VIOLA: Something light, far away.

HAMLET: The thing I used to get wrapped up in was
women.

VIOLA: If only there was a woman here, right?

HAMLET: You in love with anyone Cesario?

VIOLA: Someone who doesn't even know my name.

HAMLET: I'm sorry.

VIOLA: Don't be. It's like loving a star. You'll never
reach it, but you feel lucky to be able to look up and see
it there.

HAMLET: Your talking about love makes me wish there
was a woman I could hold.

VIOLA: Can I tell you the truth, Hamlet?

HAMLET: You couldn't tell me anything but the truth,
Cesario. Everyone's been lying to me. Family, closest
friends. It's brought me this close to killing myself.
But I feel like I can count on you for total honesty. You
were saying?

VIOLA: I was going to say, I hear women.

HAMLET: This way. Quick.

(HAMLET *leads* VIOLA *behind the rock.* CLEOPATRA *and* JULIET *enter,* CLEOPATRA *clinging to* JULIET*'s arm, dragging her around.*)

CLEOPATRA: *(Calls)* Anthony.

JULIET: You're hurting my arm.

CLEOPATRA: Shh. I hear him calling for me, "Cleopatra".

JULIET: At last I get your name. I'm Juliet.

CLEOPATRA: *(Calls)* Anthony.

JULIET: We're surrounded by so much water, not even my parents could find us here.

CLEOPATRA: What other people can do has nothing to do with Anthony. He's so far beyond anything I can explain, anything you could dream of, now he's gone, there's nothing beautiful or good anywhere.

JULIET: I've never felt like that about anyone. My parents wanted me to meet someone at a party they're having tonight, but when I stopped to rinse my hands in a fountain the water wrapped around me, carried me here.

CLEOPATRA: I was on a ship when the storm hit. There was a war going on, or something. What is that sick force in the universe that fills your life with beautiful things then takes them away one at a time.

JULIET: There is a force out there, but it moves you around for a reason. When the water lifted me up I saw my life for the first time. My parents are insane, always screaming. I have no idea why. And I don't care any more. I'm free.

CLEOPATRA: I am so fucking happy for you Juliet. *(Calls)* Anthony.

JULIET: I'll go with you but let go of my arm.

(CLEOPATRA *and* JULIET *go off.* HAMLET *and* VIOLA *come out from behind the rock.)*

HAMLET: You were right, Cesario. A minute ago everything was dark, now there's light pouring in, this incredible person.

VIOLA: She still loves Anthony.

HAMLET: Not Cleopatra, she's angry, confused.

VIOLA: Like you.

HAMLET: Like I was. But Juliet is so brave, she can take in this awful situation and find so much hope.

VIOLA: Huh.

HAMLET: You like Cleopatra? She's beautiful, right?

VIOLA: Yes but no.

HAMLET: I hope you're not saving yourself for that person who doesn't know your name.

VIOLA: I feel what I feel, what can I say.

HAMLET: They're coming back. *(Heading behind the rock)* This way.

(HAMLET *and* VIOLA *go back behind the rock.* CLEOPATRA *comes out, collapses, hugs her knees, shuts her eyes, sits in silence.* JULIET *follows.)*

JULIET: Here's not there, he's not here. Come on get up. I need to look for food but I don't want to leave you alone.

(HAMLET *comes out followed by* VIOLA.)

HAMLET: I'm Hamlet.

VIOLA: Cesario.

CLEOPATRA: I'm visualizing someone so much better than either of you. Shhh. *(She sits there in silence.)*

HAMLET: You were saying you wanted food. There's a man giving out fruit. I'll find him or get you something to eat myself.

(HAMLET *goes,* VIOLA *follows, she returns.)*

VIOLA: Hamlet wants to know if you'd like to go with him. I'll stay with Cleopatra.

JULIET: Your friend Hamlet is weird. He comes this close to me, runs away, sends you to ask for me, and now he's standing behind a tree spying on me. Why.

VIOLA: He's shaken up by the storm, like everyone is except you, and he's intimidated by you. Don't act like you don't know what I'm talking about. You're young and confident and beautiful and that gives you power. Listen. Juliet. He's a brilliant, thoughtful person. You have two perfectly fine legs, walk with him.

JULIET: *(Calls)* Hamlet.

(HAMLET *enters.)*

JULIET: *(To* HAMLET) I'd like to look around the island with Cesario. Would you stay with Cleopatra?

VIOLA: I'll stay with Cleopatra.

JULIET: *(To* VIOLA) You and I were having a conversation I wanted to finish.

HAMLET: Why don't we all go?

JULIET: I shouldn't leave her alone.

(FALSTAFF, *off, moans.)*

HAMLET: *(Calls)* Falstaff

(FALSTAFF *enters, zipping up.)*

FALSTAFF: *(To* VIOLA) No luck, too tense, I kept tugging and tugging— *(Sees the women)* Oh.

HAMLET: Juliet, Cleopatra, Falstaff.

FALSTAFF: So now's the part where you get used to my looks. I'll just stand here and sweat.

HAMLET: We're going to look for food. Could you stay with Cleopatra?

FALSTAFF: Sure.

JULIET: We'll be right back.

(HAMLET, JULIET, VIOLA *exit*. FALSTAFF *regards* CLEOPATRA *in silence, then:*)

FALSTAFF: Could I run my fingers up and down the air around your legs? I wouldn't touch you, my hands would be three feet away the whole time, I'd just go up and down your legs very fast you could keep your eyes closed the whole time sleep right through it. No? Never mind.

CLEOPATRA: I'd kill myself but I'm too sad.

FALSTAFF: You're in luck. When people spend time with me they end up laughing.

CLEOPATRA: Why.

FALSTAFF: Because I'm stupid and ugly.

CLEOPATRA: You don't have any admirable qualities do you.

FALSTAFF: No and I don't want any. Bravery gets you beat up. Patriotism gets you killed.

CLEOPATRA: The idea of a country is ridiculous.

FALSTAFF: Wisdom is annoying. Confidence is boring. What I hate most is pride in your accomplishments. Or respect. Being respected. So what.

CLEOPATRA: You're still going to drop dead for no reason.

FALSTAFF: If everybody thinks you're a piece of shit you can't let that ruin your breakfast.

(CLEOPATRA *and* FALSTAFF *sit there.*)

CLEOPATRA: Do you want to go into the woods and fuck?

FALSTAFF: Yes.

CLEOPATRA: You can't tell anyone.

(CLEOPATRA *and* FALSTAFF *go into the woods.* PROSPERO *enters, counts.*)

PROSPERO: One two three four five six. Witch.

(PROSPERO *waves his stick.* WITCH *enters.*)

WITCH: You can't keep calling me back, Prospero. My sisters and me are giving a group of soldiers a whole new kind of mental illness. It takes intense concentration.

PROSPERO: There are only six.

WITCH: You only asked for six.

PROSPERO: You said if I asked for six there would be seven.

WITCH: I had a feeling that if you picked out six there would be seven, and like all my weird hunches it was right. One of the six disguised herself as a man.

PROSPERO: One of them...

WITCH: Disguised herself.

PROSPERO: Disguised...

WITCH: I can't fucking believe you. I've been watching them from a pit on the other side of the planet, looking into images in the eyeball of an owl, you're sitting on that hill ten feet away and you can't even follow what the hell is going on.

PROSPERO: One of the men...

WITCH: If you're too senile to follow the story, you'll never be entertained and I'll never be free.

PROSPERO: The one who

WITCH: She's a woman dressed as a man.

PROSPERO: The one with the brother.

WITCH: She lost her brother, she's dressed as a man.

PROSPERO: You said there would be seven.

WITCH: You're old. Go back to your daughter so she can take care of you. I'll drop you off, let's go.

PROSPERO: I don't have a daughter.

WITCH: Yes you do, but she started listening to her husband instead of you and she wouldn't say I love you with the right intonation so you had a fucking fit and stormed off, literally. You came back to this island where you worked your magic all those years ago, so you could get back the old magic, make the greatest drama of all time, something to entertain you and make your senility bearable, but you've thrown away your book of spells and can't remember them, so when you tried to summon a spirit to carry out your project, instead of some cute sprite you got me, a fucking witch.

PROSPERO: Those aren't the six I ordered.

WITCH: But I don't make charming entertainment do I? I pluck out people's eyelashes, spit worms up their assholes, crawl into their brains and go berserk, so this assignment of bringing characters together to entertain you really goes against the grain.

PROSPERO: They're not the ones I ordered.

WITCH: Like hell they're not.

PROSPERO: When I looked into your robe

WITCH: When I opened my robe you looked into the flame in there, saw images of the most dramatic people, picked your six favorites, I ripped them from their lives, dragged them kicking and screaming over the water, and now I'm done, finished, and so sick of your shit.

PROSPERO: They don't feel right together.

WITCH: Of course they don't feel right together. They come from completely different places and times. What were you thinking?

PROSPERO: They were all made by the same creator. They should work together.

WITCH: What fairy tale do you live in?

PROSPERO: More needs to happen, make them do more together.

WITCH: I can chop off a toe, put out an eye, but as far as the overall course, once it's in motion, you just have to let them do what they're going to do.

(PROSPERO *raises his staff,* WITCH's *body freezes.*)

PROSPERO: Get in there.

WITCH: Fine. I'll make something happen, that will lead to something, that will change absolutely nothing, for your viewing pleasure. *(Wraps her cape around herself, gestures for* PROSPERO *to step aside)* I'm invisible, you're not.

(As IAGO *enters,* PROSPERO *steps aside.)*

IAGO: *(To himself)* Hamlet and Cesario are all over Juliet, but Cleopatra sounds even better.

(WITCH *speaks into* IAGO's *ear, though he can't see her.*)

WITCH: Cleopatra's that way. Go.

(IAGO *exits in the direction* CLEOPATRA *went.* PROSPERO *steps out.)*

PROSPERO: So he'll find the big one and the woman together.

WITCH: It would have happened eventually, or some other idiotic thing would have happened leading to some other pointless outcome. So get back on the hill and watch your inane drama, I'm going back to my sisters.

PROSPERO: Stay. I don't want to keep calling you.

WITCH: Oh come on Prospero. It's bad enough you make me do this shit. Don't make me watch it.

(WITCH *starts off,* PROSPERO *raises the stick. She freezes.*)

PROSPERO: You can go when it's done. *(He lowers the stick.)*

(WITCH *hisses at* PROSPERO.)

(PROSPERO *and* WITCH *go, as* HAMLET, JULIET, VIOLA *enter,* VIOLA *cutting into a coconut with* HAMLET's *knife.*)

HAMLET: Just stick the knife through the shell, Cesario.

JULIET: He's doing fine.

HAMLET: I didn't mean it as a criticism.

VIOLA: No, Hamlet's right I'm weak.

JULIET: Cesario, you're such a great friend to Hamlet. Every word he says you defend. No one's ever done that for me.

HAMLET: Your parents were so awful Juliet but you came through with amazing strength.

JULIET: Why do you keep praising me every ten seconds? It's condescending.

HAMLET: I'm being supportive which is exactly what you were saying you love when Cesario does it.

JULIET: Cesario deeply admires you, that's why he's always trying to make you sound great.

VIOLA: I'm not trying to do anything, he really does have an incredible mind.

JULIET: See?

HAMLET: Really Cesario, stop.

(IAGO *enters, throws his sack, kicks it.*)

HAMLET: Are you all right Iago?

IAGO: I have things I have to do.

(IAGO *picks up his sack, goes.*)

JULIET: He really doesn't want to be here.

HAMLET: Who does.

JULIET: I do, because of the people.

HAMLET: Me too.

VIOLA: Me too.

HAMLET: Doesn't it feel like there's a mind behind it all that brought us together?

JULIET: There is a force out there that holds you in its palm.

HAMLET: I think it leaves you alone to get the shit kicked out of you til you find your way into a current and sort of drift.

JULIET: What do you think Cesario?

VIOLA: I think the universe shits on me but it gives me great friends. Then it takes them away. But new ones seem to keep coming.

HAMLET: Isn't this where we left Cleopatra and Falstaff?

JULIET: She must be looking for Anthony on the beach.

VIOLA: You two go ahead.

JULIET: Why do you keep you trying to get away from us Cesario?

VIOLA: This shirt is itching, I'll see if Iago has another one.

HAMLET: *(To* JULIET) He'll catch up with us.

JULIET: *(To* VIOLA) Don't be long.

(HAMLET *and* JULIET *exit.)*

VIOLA: The two of them together. I can't take it.

(HAMLET *comes out.)*

HAMLET: I know why you're staying away.

VIOLA: You do.

HAMLET: You want me to finally tell Juliet how I feel about her.

VIOLA: That's it.

HAMLET: I love you, my friend.

(HAMLET *hugs* VIOLA, *goes.)*

VIOLA: I could stay here and wait for the details of their love making, or I could walk and walk, all the way to the other side of the island, where there are different people, or none.

(VIOLA *goes.* JULIET *comes out followed by* HAMLET.)

JULIET: You need to stop putting your hands on me and breathing on me, Hamlet.

HAMLET: Oh Juliet, since I landed here I've been this bizarre version of who I actually am, I'm trying to squirm back into my self but it keeps slipping away so I have to touch you or scream to give you some fucking idea who I am.

JULIET: I see who you are and it's just not for me.

HAMLET: Juliet.

(HAMLET *grabs* JULIET *and kisses her.)*

JULIET: Get off me.

(HAMLET *steps back from* JULIET.)

JULIET: Find Cleopatra. Give her this fruit. Now.

(HAMLET *takes the coconut, goes.*)

JULIET: When Hamlet grabbed me just now I felt a rush of love. For Cesario. He's so aware, of what's inside me. I'm naked before him. I have to tell him I love him this second.

(JULIET *goes off to one side. On from the other side comes* SEBASTIAN—*played by the actress who plays* VIOLA, *wearing a different shirt.*)

SEBASTIAN: My sister was standing right next to me on the ship, the water took her straight up like a toy. I'm so alone.

(JULIET *comes out.*)

JULIET: Shh. Listen. Ugh. Anyway, I love you, I love you so much. You're this dear tender thing I want to hold in my hand and keep close to me every second, I'm scaring you, I should act shy, I'll act shy, I can't act shy I'm burning up but the flames soft and cool are washing my entire body these words pouring straight from my soul I've never felt this before I'm sorry I'm spitting it's just that though I've known you for a minute it feels like every second of my life you've been watching me I'm scared to death to stop talking because I have no idea what you'll do, don't go, don't move, let's be together, our hands our bodies, let's not even use words no names just our breathing our pulse I want to be totally with you in the forest right now.

SEBASTIAN: All right.

JULIET: I like the new shirt.

(JULIET *and* SEBASTIAN *go off.* HAMLET *comes out from behind a tree on the left side of the stage, watches them go, puts down the coconut.* IAGO *peeks out from behind a bush on the right side of the stage, watches* HAMLET.)

HAMLET: Saving yourself for someone you'll never have, are you Cesario? There's no one on this planet I can trust.

(IAGO *enters.)*

IAGO: The nicer somebody is to you, the worse they're about to abuse you.

HAMLET: Oh Iago. I'm so disgusted with the human race.

IAGO: So you've heard about Falstaff.

HAMLET: Heard what.

IAGO: He's been slipping people these drugs he makes from plants.

HAMLET: *(Laughs)* Falstaff?

IAGO: You haven't noticed anybody acting weird all of a sudden?

HAMLET: Cesario turned into a lying shit, but—

IAGO: Hmmm.

HAMLET: Hmm what.

IAGO: You're already upset. This isn't the time.

HAMLET: For what.

IAGO: For you to see the effect of Falstaff's drugs on Cleopatra.

HAMLET: What effects? Iago?

IAGO: Walk that way. Quietly. Go.

(HAMLET *exits.* IAGO *waits.* HAMLET *enters, stands there.)*

HAMLET: Wow.

IAGO: He hasn't offered you anything has he?

HAMLET: No.

IAGO: Then I guess it was some stupid joke I didn't get.

HAMLET: What joke.

IAGO: When I was giving Falstaff some fruit before he pointed to you and said tomorrow morning we can kick you, poke your eyes, but you'll never get up, ever.

HAMLET: You're fucking with me.

(HAMLET *shoves* IAGO *to the ground.*)

IAGO: Forget trying to help, I've got work to do. *(He starts off.)*

HAMLET: Iago. I'm sorry. It's just, I've had this voice telling me something deadly is out there, do something about it, but whenever I do the consequences are so awful I can't think about them without wanting to kill myself.

IAGO: You're right to be careful, Hamlet. You shouldn't do anything about Falstaff unless you're sure.

HAMLET: Right.

IAGO: Luckily there's a way to be sure. The tree over by the clearing? At the base there are a few little green plants with shiny leaves. That's snake root. It's poisonous. That's what Falstaff said he was going to give you.

HAMLET: So I can just check around the tree.

IAGO: If the little plants are still there, you have nothing to worry about.

(HAMLET *goes.*)

IAGO: I'm fairly sure the plants aren't there, because they're here. *(He takes out plants. He opens the coconut, adds water and leaves from the plants, stirs.)* I was going to use them to make Falstaff throw up, but this new idea is so much bigger and better. *(Dashes into the woods, calls)* Falstaff.

(IAGO *comes back out as* FALSTAFF *comes running out.*)

FALSTAFF: What Iago what?

IAGO: Hamlet's having these terrible fits of depression.

FALSTAFF: I'm so sorry.

IAGO: I was going to give him this fruit drink to cheer him up then I thought it should come from you because you're his favorite person here.

FALSTAFF: I guess Hamlet likes me more than I thought. Usually people like me less than I thought.

IAGO: He'll be here in a minute. Don't tell anybody else about his problem, he's very private.

FALSTAFF: Okay.

IAGO: And remember, the drink is from you. (*He goes.*)

FALSTAFF: Iago thinks of everything.

(CLEOPATRA *comes out.*)

CLEOPATRA: Come on back into the woods.

FALSTAFF: I need to do something for somebody first.

CLEOPATRA: What?

FALSTAFF: I promised I wouldn't tell.

CLEOPATRA: What's this drink?

FALSTAFF: I'll just be a minute.

CLEOPATRA: Who besides Iago does this have to do with?

(FALSTAFF *is silent.*)

CLEOPATRA: Do you realize that where I come from people would organize their entire month around a chance to be anywhere near me just to say something stupid in passing, and if I'd happen to stop and exchange a few words with somebody he'd start stuttering and perspire and go tell everyone he'd ever

met and write about it and I don't mean just letters
or diary entrees I mean epic poems and plays or
he'd devote his life to making massive sculptures or
paintings or stadiums.

FALSTAFF: Keeping my word to my friends is the one
pretentious virtue in which I indulge.

CLEOPATRA: *(Covers her eyes)* Shit. I'm completely in
love with you. Nothing from before seems real.

FALSTAFF: Me too, but

CLEOPATRA: It's okay. I trust you. I'll be waiting.

(CLEOPATRA *embraces* FALSTAFF, *goes.)*

FALSTAFF: *(To himself)* Don't you dare get your hopes
up, you fat idiot. Any second she'll come back to
reality and devote the rest of her life to ignoring you.
I'm so tired of scraping you off the floor.

(HAMLET *enters, stares at* FALSTAFF.)

FALSTAFF: *(To* HAMLET) Hamlet.

HAMLET: Who are you.

FALSTAFF: Your friend, Falstaff. You all right?

HAMLET: Funny.

FALSTAFF: What.

HAMLET: It seems like you really do give a shit about
me.

FALSTAFF: After knowing you for three seconds I
wanted to be you. There's something about you I root
for.

HAMLET: Falstaff. I believe you.

FALSTAFF: Oh good. So here's this fruit drink I made
you. Drink.

HAMLET: You drink.

FALSTAFF: It's for you.

(HAMLET's *entire body trembles, he hunches over.*)

HAMLET: I'll drink it if you leave me alone.

FALSTAFF: Okay.

(FALSTAFF *leaves.*)

(HAMLET *hugs himself, rocks.*)

(IAGO *enters.*)

HAMLET: He tried to get me to drink this. It has the leaves in it.

IAGO: So from now on be careful what you drink.

HAMLET: There's nothing else I can do?

IAGO: This conversation is making me nervous. *(He starts off.)*

HAMLET: Wait. Iago.

(HAMLET *follows* IAGO *off, as* JULIET *and* SEBASTIAN *enter.*)

JULIET: When I said your name why did you start up with some joke?

SEBASTIAN: I wasn't making a joke, you didn't say my name.

(HAMLET *comes back, sees* JULIET *and* SEBASTIAN, *hides.*)

JULIET: I said Cesario.

SEBASTIAN: And I said I'm Sebastian.

JULIET: Were we getting too close so you had to start acting strange?

SEBASTIAN: I'm not acting strange, you are.

JULIET: I suddenly feel like we don't know each other, it's scaring me.

SEBASTIAN: You feel like we don't know each other because this is our first conversation.

JULIET: The things we said before meant so much to me.

SEBASTIAN: We didn't say anything before because you never let me speak.

JULIET: I never let you speak?

SEBASTIAN: Not two words.

JULIET: What about when you said I was confident and beautiful?

SEBASTIAN: When did I say you were confident and beautiful?

JULIET: So since the second you got your body on top of me none of the things you said count.

SEBASTIAN: I don't know what you want from me, tell me what you want.

JULIET: I want you to talk to me like before so there's some trace of continuity, it's not like we're animals.

SEBASTIAN: I get it, it's because I'm not big.

JULIET: What does your size have to do with anything?

SEBASTIAN: I'm not really tall so you think you can drag me off to have sex then get me to say yes to whatever insanity comes out of your mouth, this always happens.

JULIET: Drag you off to have sex?

SEBASTIAN: I may not have hair all over my chest but I know when I'm being pushed around.

JULIET: I don't want to push you around, I don't want to look at you. Where are you going?

SEBASTIAN: You said you don't want to look at me.

JULIET: That you remember.

(SEBASTIAN *goes.*)

JULIET: You think you know someone.

(HAMLET *comes out.*)

HAMLET: It's not his fault that he's not himself, Juliet.

JULIET: You're spying on me again, get out.

(SEBASTIAN *comes out, pulls* HAMLET *away from* JULIET.)

HAMLET: Cesario.

SEBASTIAN: I'm Sebastian.

HAMLET: Sebastian, okay, I was telling Juliet about this thing we need to do something about, we'll need your help, to stop this person—

JULIET: I can't deal with your shit right now Hamlet.

HAMLET: Now is all we have, we have to work fast, for all our sakes, listen.

(*As* HAMLET *leads* JULIET *and* SEBASTIAN *off to the side,* PROSPERO *and* WITCH *enter.*)

PROSPERO: So now they'll take that stupid lie seriously?

WITCH: From the way their eyebrows are twitching I'd say yes.

PROSPERO: It's too crazy.

WITCH: What do you expect? It was conceived by a senile lunatic on a particularly delusional day.

PROSPERO: Make it less crazy.

WITCH: I can't.

PROSPERO: Then I will.

WITCH: You'll step in and tell them everything, send us all home early?

PROSPERO: If they keep going wrong I'll reveal things, tell them I'm a wise, friar or… (*Thinks*)

(WITCH *snores.*)

(HAMLET *returns with* JULIET *and* SEBASTIAN. WITCH *leads* PROSPERO *off.*)

SEBASTIAN: What you're saying does make sense of things.

JULIET/SEBASTIAN: *(To* HAMLET) The way he's acting./ *(To* HAMLET) The way she's acting.

JULIET: But why would Falstaff want to hurt us?

SEBASTIAN: You can't figure out insanity. You have to just do something about it.

HAMLET: *(To* JULIET) So you're convinced?

JULIET: *(Starts off)* I should see what he's done to Cleopatra.

SEBASTIAN: I would think you'd feel safer going in there with me.

JULIET: I'm just going to look, I won't get close, I didn't say you couldn't come. Is this about your height again?

SEBASTIAN: If you're going then go.

(JULIET *goes.)*

SEBASTIAN: You look at me like you know me.

HAMLET: You remind me of a friend I'm worried about.

SEBASTIAN: I'm missing someone I lost who really knew me.

HAMLET: I wonder if I'll ever see my friend again the way he was.

SEBASTIAN: I wonder if you can ever appreciate someone you love when they're standing right there.

HAMLET: You talk ideas, feelings, like the conversation will go on forever.

SEBASTIAN: But it doesn't.

HAMLET: And those things you could say to that one person become a poetry that's gone from the world.

SEBASTIAN: You're saying random phrases to yourself that no one understands.

(HAMLET *kisses* SEBASTIAN. SEBASTIAN *backs off.)*

HAMLET: I don't know why I did that, I'm sorry.

SEBASTIAN: It happens.

(JULIET *comes out, embraces* SEBASTIAN.)

JULIET: Her body's moving like she's not in control of it.

SEBASTIAN: We'll go in there and confront Falstaff, and see how he reacts.

(IAGO *appears behind the rock, speaks only to* HAMLET.)

IAGO: *(Offers rope)* This could go around Falstaff's throat, drag him into the water til he tells you the truth.

(HAMLET *takes the long piece.)*

HAMLET: Thanks, Iago.

IAGO: And there's always your knife.

HAMLET: My knife.

IAGO: *(To* HAMLET) Let me get Cleopatra out of your way first. Hold on.

(IAGO *exits.* HAMLET *regards* JULIET *and* SEBASTIAN *embracing, regards the knife, waits. Offstage sounds)*

HAMLET: Let's go around this way.

(HAMLET, JULIET, *and* SEBASTIAN *exit, as* IAGO *enters followed by* CLEOPATRA.)

IAGO: It looked like you were with somebody. Were you with somebody?

CLEOPATRA: What do you want.

IAGO: To introduce myself, give you some fruit.

CLEOPATRA: I'm not hungry.

IAGO: You look like you could use some energy.

CLEOPATRA: What?

IAGO: You seem depleted. Like you need a more energy.

CLEOPATRA: What the fuck are you saying?

(IAGO *shrugs.*)

CLEOPATRA: Actually, give me a couple of those.

IAGO: You weren't hungry. Now you're eating for two.

CLEOPATRA: You going to give me the fruit?

(IAGO *doesn't move.*)

CLEOPATRA: So…

IAGO: What will you give me?

CLEOPATRA: What will I give you?

(IAGO *stands there.* CLEOPATRA *laughs at him. He grabs her.*)

CLEOPATRA: Get the fuck off me.

(PROSPERO *comes forward.*)

PROSPERO: *(Announces)* I saw. Everything.

(IAGO *flees.*)

PROSPERO: I'll tell everyone everything. The big one is good. The one who said he's bad is a liar.

CLEOPATRA: Who are you?

PROSPERO: I, we

(HAMLET, JULIET, SEBASTIAN *enter, covered in blood.* HAMLET *holds out his bloody knife.*)

JULIET: So much blood it kept coming.

SEBASTIAN: I was holding his arm, he wouldn't stop moving.

HAMLET: I killed him.

(IAGO *appears behind the rock, watches.*)

IAGO: *(Aside)* To have an idea brought to life, more completely than you ever imagined, is so gratifying.

CLEOPATRA: Who did you kill?

JULIET: To save you.

SEBASTIAN: And all of us.

HAMLET: Falstaff.

CLEOPATRA: Where is he?

SEBASTIAN: In there.

(CLEOPATRA *runs off.*)

HAMLET: What we did was right. Remember.

(CLEOPATRA, *off, screams.*)

IAGO: *(To* HAMLET*)* I'll get a drink that will calm her down.

(IAGO *goes as* CLEOPATRA *returns.*)

CLEOPATRA: You cut him up.

SEBASTIAN: We had to do something.

HAMLET: Iago will explain.

CLEOPATRA: Iago?

HAMLET: He told me how Falstaff was trying to kill me.

JULIET: We saw what Falstaff was doing to you.

SEBASTIAN: We know how he drugged you.

CLEOPATRA: *(Rages)* What's going on in your heads has nothing to do with reality.

HAMLET: She'll hurt herself, where's the rope.

SEBASTIAN: I've got her.

JULIET: Hold still.

(JULIET *and* SEBASTIAN *help* HAMLET *restrain* CLEOPATRA. PROSPERO *steps forward with staff raised. All freeze.* WITCH *observes.*)

PROSPERO: I Prospero had this witch bring you here to make a story so great that my life would feel better.

(IAGO *appears with drink, unseen.*)

IAGO: *(Aside)* Every now and then I allow myself the delusion that I have some control over things but I don't I have no control. *(He exits.)*

PROSPERO: But the order of who met who and what they said led you to trust someone bad and kill someone good it all went wrong I'm sorry.

(PROSPERO *lets down his arms. The others unfreeze and scream at* PROSPERO *all at once.*)

CLEOPATRA: *(Scream at once)* How could you let it happen you just stood there

SEBASTIAN: *(Scream at once)* How could you take me from my sister in that storm

HAMLET: *(Scream at once)* Why didn't you do anything once you could see what we were doing

JULIET: *(Scream at once)* That awful storm the water dragging us all here just because

(PROSPERO *brings the stick back up, they freeze.*)

WITCH: I'll take them back where they came from, it's on my way.

PROSPERO: Or we could help them work together to punish the liar.

(IAGO *comes out with rope, puts it around* PROSPERO's *throat, the others remain frozen.*)

IAGO: I have a better idea for an ending. Keep the staff raised and you can see it.

(PROSPERO *gasps for air.*)

WITCH: *(To* IAGO*)* I was heading out, let me drop you off.

IAGO: First take the knife from Hamlet's hand, bring Cleopatra to that low rock.

(WITCH *takes knife from* HAMLET's *hand, brings* CLEOPATRA *off.*)

WITCH: *(To herself)* I've been enslaved by another shithead with a vision.

IAGO: Press her back against the rock so the jagged part's digging into her head.

WITCH: *(Off)* Done.

IAGO: Cut out her tongue.

(CLEOPATRA, *off, gasps.*)

(Tongue flies onstage. WITCH *enters.)*

WITCH: All right then?

IAGO: Take Cesario over to that patch of dirt by the tree.

WITCH: He's not Ces— Never mind.

(WITCH *leads* SEBASTIAN *off.*)

IAGO: Press his face in the dirt.

WITCH: *(Off)* Your choices are weird without being the least bit interesting.

(SEBASTIAN, *off, gasps.*)

IAGO: Leave him lying there breathing in dirt.

(VIOLA *appears off to the side.*)

VIOLA: *(Aside)* The world can get so much worse, so quickly.

(VIOLA *hides.* WITCH *returns.*)

WITCH: Any more quirky inspirations?

IAGO: Put out Hamlet's eyes with your thumbs.

WITCH: I'll scoop them out with the knife.

IAGO: No. Drop the knife.

(WITCH *drops the knife.* VIOLA *steps out, unseen, picks up the knife.*)

IAGO: Use your hands. Put your thumbs on his eyes and push.

(VIOLA *stabs* IAGO, *who falls.* PROSPERO *lowers his arms, the others come unfrozen.*)

IAGO: I'm fine. (*He crawls behind a bush, dies.*)

WITCH: I'll sew Cleopatra's tongue back on.

PROSPERO: Do it. Fast.

WITCH: I was just following his orders like I follow yours. (*She picks up tongue, exits.*)

HAMLET: (*To* VIOLA) How did you do that Cesario? I mean Sebastian.

VIOLA: Something came over me. Was it right? Did you call me Sebastian?

JULIET: Of course it was right. Iago lied to get us to kill Falstaff.

HAMLET: You don't remember wanting to be called Sebastian?

VIOLA: You killed who?

JULIET: You don't remember what we did to Falstaff?

VIOLA: Who said I wanted to be called Sebastian?

CLEOPATRA: (*Off*) Get your fingers off my tongue.

WITCH: I should have sewn it to your ass.

(CLEOPATRA *enters followed by* WITCH.)

CLEOPATRA: (*To* VIOLA) How'd you get there so fast? You were just wiping dirt off your face over there.

(HAMLET *and* JULIET *look off stage.*)

JULIET: He's still wiping dirt off his face over there.

HAMLET: Cesario. There are two of you.

(VIOLA *looks off.*)

VIOLA: It's you. You think you're staring at yourself. I'm not you. I'm someone who hid because everything was out of control, everything is out of control, but if the insanity brings me back to you I'll put up with all the ridiculous shit the universe can throw at me. *(Reveals herself)* I'm Viola. Hug me, my brother. *(She hurries off.)*

PROSPERO: So the six did become seven.

WITCH: Fuck if I'm not always right.

JULIET: *(To off)* Which of you did I go into the forest with?

(SEBASTIAN *comes out.*)

SEBASTIAN: That was me.

JULIET: So all those things you said that made no sense

SEBASTIAN: Made perfect sense. And when you got mad at me for no reason

JULIET: I had a reason.

SEBASTIAN: But when you went into the forest with me, you thought I was someone else.

JULIET: Someone who said I'm beautiful and confident, which you never did.

SEBASTIAN: My sister and I have similar tastes. She's always expressing things I feel very deeply.

JULIET: Well then, since it was your feelings your sister was expressing, when I went into the forest thinking I was with your sister, it really was you I was thinking I was with.

SEBASTIAN: So we really did love each other from the moment we met.

JULIET: And even before.

(JULIET *and* SEBASTIAN *embrace, exit together.*)

(JULIET, *off, sighs, gasps, kissing.*)

(VIOLA *backs on, watching the off-stage lovers.*)

HAMLET: Viola.

VIOLA: Hamlet. You look sad. Because it's not you with Juliet?

HAMLET: No, because you're the most incredible friend I've ever had, but you're standing there alone, watching your brother with Juliet, thinking about that person who doesn't know your name.

VIOLA: He does know my name now. But he'll never love me, unless you love me.

HAMLET: *(Sad)* Oh. *(Happy)* Oh. Well then, for a friend.

(HAMLET *kisses* VIOLA, *they embrace.*)

WITCH: The lovers are fucking. We're done.

CLEOPATRA: It's not a happy ending for Falstaff.

HAMLET: Or for me. I close my eyes and see Falstaff reaching towards me like this.

(JULIET *enters.*)

JULIET: I washed off his blood but I still feel it all over me. Sebastian's pacing, he won't talk to me.

VIOLA: Maybe after so much bad there can't be a happy ending.

PROSPERO: If there's…any way I can make one—

CLEOPATRA: Bring back Falstaff.

JULIET: That would make up for everything you've done to us.

HAMLET: Everything we've done to each other.

PROSPERO: When someone's dead there's nothing I can do.

VIOLA: (*To* WITCH) What about you?

WITCH: Nothing can be done for the dead (*Suddenly writhes, moans, has a vision*) except a play.

CLEOPATRA: A play?

HAMLET: A play can help us see more deeply.

VIOLA: Give us hope.

CLEOPATRA: Doing a play can make you feel nice but it can't move a fingernail or a hair or actually do anything.

WITCH: It can and will.

PROSPERO: Her visions are always right.

JULIET: Let's at least try.

CLEOPATRA: After what's happened, doing a play would feel ridiculous.

VIOLA: That we're here is ridiculous, that we found each other is ridiculous.

HAMLET: To think you can know the limits of what's possible anywhere ever is ridiculous.

CLEOPATRA: Fine. We'll do a play.

JULIET: What should it be about?

WITCH: Don't ask don't think go go.

(*They sing, dance, as necessary.* WITCH *waves her arms to make music.*)

(JULIET *wails.*)

(CLEOPATRA *moans.*)

(HAMLET *screams.*)

(VIOLA *sighs.*)

(PROSPERO *whines.*)

(WITCH *waves her arms so their crying out reverberates and becomes louder.* FALSTAFF *appears behind the rock. The others see* FALSTAFF *and become silent.* WITCH *stops the music and lights.*)

HAMLET: Is that who I think it is?

CLEOPATRA: If it is there's nothing but nonsense beneath the sky, thank god.

FALSTAFF: What a dream I was having. These ghosts of my friends all colliding in one point. I heard them, followed the sounds.

HAMLET: Iago told us terrible things about you. But Prospero who had us all brought here by this witch told us Iago was lying.

JULIET: Now Iago's dead.

CLEOPATRA: Like we thought you were.

FALSTAFF: Oh no I just tripped or bumped into somebody, smacked my head on something, got some sleep.

CLEOPATRA: You're covered in blood.

FALSTAFF: That's berries. I stuffed them in my shirt to give Cleopatra.

HAMLET: I felt the knife going through your skin.

JULIET: I saw blood, I thought. It happened so fast.

CLEOPATRA: Your body was all over. A piece of you here, a piece there.

FALSTAFF: That's how I always look when I'm lying down.

HAMLET: Falstaff. When I confronted you in the forest it was like my actions were these wild dogs going in all directions, I could see them but I had no control.

JULIET: We had a fever. We were burning up.

HAMLET: I'm sorry.

JULIET: I'm sorry Falstaff.

FALSTAFF: It's all right. People get mad at me all the time. Though the stabbing is new.

JULIET: Let me get someone else who could really use your forgiveness.

VIOLA: I can't wait to see his face.

(JULIET *exits.*)

CLEOPATRA: Falstaff. I'm sorry for making you keep our being together secret. What's wrong?

FALSTAFF: You're about to tell me to get the fuck out of here.

CLEOPATRA: No I'm not.

FALSTAFF: Yes you are. You just realized I'm shit.

CLEOPATRA: No.

FALSTAFF: Then realize it already I can't stand the suspense.

CLEOPATRA: What I'm saying is I was wrong to keep our love private like it was a separate story all to itself. On this island we're all part of the same story, we can't be confused or disgusted by each other. We need to help them understand us. I need to come out and say Falstaff I love you and I don't care who knows.

(CLEOPATRA *embraces* FALSTAFF.)

VIOLA: You got a woman to hold onto after all.

FALSTAFF: Cesario?

VIOLA: I'm Viola. It's a long story. But a story we were able to keep groping through til we got ourselves a happy ending.

HAMLET: It wasn't us controlling the story, it was something beyond even what we think is out there controlling things.

FALSTAFF: It was berries that saved my life, the force that can work any miracle is food and I worship it daily.

CLEOPATRA: You put those berries in your shirt so you could give them to me. It was love that saved you, the most powerful force, driving everything.

FALSTAFF: Love is a fruit so amazing that after you eat it you want to spend the rest of your life with a tree.

CLEOPATRA: Love is all there is. The end.

(JULIET, *off, screams.*)

(JULIET *comes out.*)

JULIET: I was hugging Sebastian, he flew out of my arms and over the sea.

WITCH: He bounced back to his other life. Time's up.

VIOLA: Sebastian's gone?

WITCH: You will be too any minute.

PROSPERO: Things my magic does don't last.

VIOLA: Being separated from people you love, it never stops.

JULIET: Can I go where Sebastian is?

PROSPERO: You each go right back to the time and place we borrowed you from.

JULIET: So you meet someone, feel this rush, run off together, suddenly feel like you're strangers, struggle to get back where you started, think you made it, come up against a wall, bang your heads against it, finally figure everything out, hug as hard as you can, go flying apart, and that's love?

CLEOPATRA: When you're older you skip some of the steps.

HAMLET: I can't go back to what I left, not yet.

CLEOPATRA: Not ever.

FALSTAFF: *(To* CLEOPATRA*)* I'll always remember this feeling of you holding me.

WITCH: You won't remember any of this.

PROSPERO: Maybe in a dream.

JULIET: If Sebastian's not there I'll never love anybody.

WITCH: Yes you will.

JULIET: Never like that.

WITCH: Exactly like that.

CLEOPATRA: So I'll go back to that pathetic love I thought was the greatest ever?

WITCH: And swear it's the greatest ever.

VIOLA: Will I find my brother again?

WITCH: And lose him again.

HAMLET: Will I make the world any better?

WITCH: A little for a time.

(IAGO *drifts on.*)

IAGO: Will I make a real difference?

WITCH: A little for a time.

(IAGO *drifts off.*)

FALSTAFF: I don't want to know what'll happen to me.

WITCH: Wise choice. It's not pretty.

JULIET: *(To* VIOLA*)* Can I hold onto you and think of your brother?

(CLEOPATRA, FALSTAFF, HAMLET, JULIET, *and* VIOLA *cling together.*)

HAMLET: *(To* VIOLA*)* I wish I realized how I felt about you sooner.

VIOLA: I wish I didn't hide who I was for so long.

JULIET: I wish we didn't waste so much time with those arguments.

FALSTAFF: I wish we could do everything we did again and again exactly the same.

CLEOPATRA: So do I.

(All drift apart and off stage, only the PROSPERO *and* WITCH *remain.)*

PROSPERO: It was you right? You saved the story?

WITCH: They said it was love, or fate. It was masochism. *(Opens her robe, reveals cuts in her skin)* I got in between Hamlet and Falstaff, took the cuts in my skin to save his. Anything to get you your happy ending, so I can finally get back to my sisters.

PROSPERO: Stay. Talk to me.

WITCH: I gave you your play, I don't have to talk to you.

PROSPERO: You do.

*(*WITCH *starts off,* PROSPERO *raises the stick, it doesn't stop her.)*

WITCH: Your stick is out of power. *(Laughs)* You don't even have a way of getting home now. Want a ride?

PROSPERO: No.

WITCH: You think you have no reason to go back, but look. *(Opens her robe)* Your daughter has a daughter. Want a ride now?

PROSPERO: I want to see the baby.

WITCH: The baby doesn't want to see you.

PROSPERO: I want to see the baby.

WITCH: Your daughter's going to keep right on ignoring you, you'll keep getting weaker and dumber til you die.

PROSPERO: I want to see the baby.

WITCH: After all the pain humanity has caused you, you still need to see its latest offering.

PROSPERO: Yes. But you won't take me, will you.

WITCH: No. *(Laughs at him. Goes)*

PROSPERO: *(To audience)* I was wrong to storm off. Drag all the others away from their lives. Maybe everything I've ever done was wrong. But I'm still living. I can keep trying to forgive, and be forgiven by, those I love. I want to see the baby. Don't leave me alone on this island. Send me home. Please clap.

END OF PLAY

COMPLETE UNKNOWNS

CHARACTERS

MOLLY *is a theater director who has been struggling for so long that she embraces the struggle itself as her career.*

ELLEN *is terrified of others, has written a play.*

The first seven scenes take place in a residence for people with psychiatric disorders, the eighth scene takes place in a hospital. But all settings can be defined by the arrangement of a couple of chairs.

1.

(MOLLY *sits smoking a cigarette.* ELLEN *stands at a distance, watching her.*)

MOLLY: Did you want to join the workshop? I saw you checking us out from down the hall.

(ELLEN *stands there.*)

MOLLY: We'll do some acting, some writing. If you're feeling creative you could give it a try.

(ELLEN *stands there.*)

MOLLY: Oh well. I'll be here every Monday if you—

(ELLEN *mumbles, inaudible.*)

MOLLY: Sorry?

(ELLEN *reaches into her clothes, pulls out pieces of paper folded together.*)

MOLLY: Ah. You've written a play.

(ELLEN *nods.*)

MOLLY: Good. It's good for the soul. Want me to give it a read?

(ELLEN *nods.*)

MOLLY: I'd love to.

(ELLEN *hands it to* MOLLY)

MOLLY: These markings mean somebody's speaking? There are two of them, right? The dash is one character the squiggle's the other?

(ELLEN *nods.*)

MOLLY: Do you want to tell me their names? Their ages? Where they are?

(ELLEN *shakes her head.*)

MOLLY: All right then. *(Reads)*

(ELLEN *watches* MOLLY *read.*)

MOLLY: Huh.

(ELLEN *trembles.*)

MOLLY: You okay?

(ELLEN *stands still, watches.*)

MOLLY: *(Reads)* I know this…conversation. I know these people. *(Looks up)* There's something here.

(ELLEN *stands there.*)

MOLLY: I'd love to work on this with the group, maybe even use it for the scene night. Did you hear me mention that we might have a scene night—

(ELLEN *nods rapidly.*)

MOLLY: But, the thing is, part of the reason Tom brought me in to do the workshop, it's not just about theater, it's also to get people in the House working together, communicating.

(ELLEN *stands there.*)

MOLLY: Which isn't really your style, is it.

(ELLEN *stands there.*)

MOLLY: Well, even if you're not sitting with us, I guess we could work on this as long as, maybe you'd listen from down the hall? Like you did today, okay?

(ELLEN *nods.*)

MOLLY: Good. I'm Molly. I'm excited to be working on your play.

2.

(ELLEN *sits sideways on a chair, clinging to it, contorted, face buried.* MOLLY *stands.*)

MOLLY: Getting feedback can be annoying, I know, I should have started off by saying people really liked your play, maybe you couldn't tell from down the hall but sitting in the circle I could feel it, from their breathing—

(ELLEN *looks up, still contorted.*)

MOLLY: Everybody was right there with it, the rhythm, the tension, you could feel it rising, so when it ended all of a sudden I wanted more—

(ELLEN *starts to bury her face, peeks out.*)

MOLLY: That's good, that means there's something there, or I wouldn't have felt so, UGH, frustrated, but I'm not saying you have to change it, I'd still want to do it if we have a scene night.

(ELLEN *looks up.*)

MOLLY: I'd do Rob's piece too, about his time in prison, and Ed's piece about Iraq—

(ELLEN *hugs her knee.*)

MOLLY: I'm not asking you to spell everything out like those guys do, I love that you leave things mysterious, but in their plays it's clear what the stakes are, the urgency. In yours there's a rhythm, it's smooth, like my dog's fur, but when I scrape his smooth fur aside I see grit and scratches and veins, I feel there's this visceral stuff in your piece but people might not get it unless you give them some clue, some moment of, eruption or—

(ELLEN *is totally contorted, face buried.*)

MOLLY: Forget it. Ellen. What you wrote is pure. It's exactly what came to you and that's sacred. It must be the worst feeling having me ask for more when you've already put out everything you've got. I get that. And I accept it. You don't have to change a single—

(ELLEN *gasps.*)

MOLLY: What.

(ELLEN *springs to her feet, takes out the script, takes out a pen, kneels on the floor, puts the script on the chair, brings pen to paper, stares at the paper, gripping pen, her face expressing horror and disgust, pants.*)

MOLLY: Rewriting can be painful, sure.

3.

(*Music plays on a portable player.* MOLLY *sits holding a bag of cookies,* ELLEN *sits beside her, takes a cookie, examines it.*)

MOLLY: Not only did he say we can have scene night, he loved the reading so much he's giving us money for costumes and props.

(ELLEN *turns away from* MOLLY, *hunches over, stuffs the cookie in her mouth, chews rapidly, turns back to* MOLLY.)

MOLLY: Your style of eating cookies is original as your writing.

(ELLEN *stops chewing.*)

MOLLY: No no, we're celebrating, go for it.

(ELLEN *resumes chewing, takes another cookie, examines it, turns away, etc*)

MOLLY: Ed and Abby are memorizing their lines, Tom's really excited, and all because one day you—

(ELLEN *shakes head.*)

MOLLY: It wasn't one day. It was weeks.

(ELLEN *shakes.*)

MOLLY: Months. Years?

(ELLEN *nods.*)

MOLLY: Three four, five years…

(ELLEN *nods, shrugs.*)

MOLLY: Of crossing things out, starting over…

(ELLEN *nods.*)

MOLLY: Staring at a blank piece of paper, at a wall…

(ELLEN *nods.*)

MOLLY: At your hands, the sky, the laundry machine…

(ELLEN *nods.*)

MOLLY: Until eventually the words came and you wrote them down and there it was.

(ELLEN *nods.*)

MOLLY: But who would bring your play to life, you—

(ELLEN *shakes.*)

MOLLY: —didn't wonder. Just tucked it away. Your own quiet secret.

(ELLEN *nods.*)

MOLLY: Until you heard about the workshop.

(ELLEN *nods.*)

MOLLY: Wondered what if.

(ELLEN *nods.*)

MOLLY: And got up your courage to give it to me.

(ELLEN *nods.*)

MOLLY: I'm so glad you did, Ellen. More cookies?

(ELLEN *takes another cookie, turns away, stuffs it in her mouth, chews.*)

MOLLY: When I was celebrating with the others they started dancing. I'm guessing that's not something you do in the company of others.

(ELLEN *shrugs.*)

MOLLY: (*Turns her chair away*) I'm not looking. Go for it.

(ELLEN *starts to dance, tentatively.*)

MOLLY: I have to tell you Ellen, your play is really getting through to me. It's this argument I've heard, I've been in, so many times.

(ELLEN's *dance intensifies.*)

MOLLY: The words are different every time. But it's always that same ridiculous nightmare of a conversation.

(ELLEN *dances slowly, stares at* MOLLY.)

MOLLY: How did you hear me? When I was breaking up with somebody. Having a fight with a friend. When my mom and dad were yelling at each other. Where were you standing? It's creepy. But it's great too. It gives me chills.

(ELLEN *stands there staring at* MOLLY.)

MOLLY: You've written an amazing play, Ellen. And it's getting done. Dance.

(ELLEN *dances with intensity.*)

4.

(MOLLY *stands,* ELLEN *sits.* MOLLY *can't escape* ELLEN's *gaze.*)

MOLLY: When I'm directing a play I get the feeling I control the world but I don't, I have no control. A tornado puts a tree through the wall of the common room and the workshop's cancelled, it just happened,

this ridiculous unpredictable thing, it's nobody's fault.
An "act of god", what does that mean. Tom needs his
whole annual budget for repairs and there we are.
The workshop didn't pay much but it paid. My job
developing plays for the Rep takes a ton of time and
pays basically nothing and I have this thing about to
land on me next month so I've taken a proofreading
job, I have to put in as many hours as possible starting
now. I need money, Ellen. I can't just keep not making
money. Tom'll have me back for the workshop some
day I'm sure. You held onto your play for years before
we met, right? I know it's different now, we got your
hopes up, it was about to get out there and now it feels
like if you die no one'll ever know about this amazing
thing but plays get put off all the time Ellen, an actor
gets a better offer, you lose the space, somebody loses
their funding, you want to kill yourself then a few
months down the road it picks right back up, well
sometimes it doesn't, you wait all summer for the call
and then find out they're doing somebody else's play
from a brochure or a website and when you call they
say well at least you got to hear it isn't it great we
did all those readings but that's not me Ellen, I said
your play would be done and it will, if I have to find
you another director no no no no that's not going to
happen, I get your play, I love it, I have to do it, and
I will. Okay? Screw the tornado. We can't use the
common room, so we'll use the lawn out back, we'll set
up chairs, there's a light out there right? We'll rehearse
at weird times, before breakfast maybe, til they clean
up the debris we'll use the basement, we'll buy our
own props or just find stuff, when will I sleep I have
no idea and then there's my health but you don't want
to hear about that, and if people say why am I doing
this play and not the others I'll say after the tornado
everybody's desperate to process what happened
and your play's about the weird rhythm of loss or

everybody's desperate to forget and escape and your play's this delightful style piece, whatever, the bottom line is, Ellen, we're doing your play. We're doing your play. That's what I came here to tell you. Why? What did you think I was going to say?

5.

(MOLLY *confronts* ELLEN, *who stands behind chairs.*)

MOLLY: No. No. Ellen. I need to know why you hate what we're doing.

(ELLEN *shakes her head.*)

MOLLY: Yes you do, it's in your face, the way you're standing.

(ELLEN *adjusts her posture.*)

MOLLY: Bullshit.

(ELLEN *stands there.*)

MOLLY: The actors'll be back in five minutes. We're going to start setting things. If you don't tell me now—

(ELLEN *hunches over, shrugs.*)

MOLLY: I won't be mad, or hurt, I can take criticism, it won't kill me.

(ELLEN *starts to gesture, drops her arms, shrinks.*)

MOLLY: Come on. Let it out.

(*In a burst of fury* ELLEN *springs up, fists clenched.*)

ELLEN: (*Barely audible*) It's too big and too loud. (*She sits, looks away.*)

MOLLY: I appreciate your input. But a play is different from a book or a movie, there's no close-ups or narrator. Everything can't be subtle, little glances, whispered thoughts, it doesn't work.

(ELLEN *sits there, looking away.*)

MOLLY: Yes the play comes from you. It's of you. But it's not for you. Everybody needs to get it. So the actors have to bring it to life a way that people can understand and feel. That's why the movement, the shouting, the big physical choices, we're taking all that energy that's in your language and… *(Thinks)* Shit. You're right. We've lost the pain.

(MOLLY *paces,* ELLEN *watches.*)

MOLLY: Mm. Okay. When the actors get back I'll tell them that what we've been doing so far was research. We found the noise. But now we're going to bury all that. On the surface, from now on, it's all quiet.

(*As* MOLLY *speaks:* ELLEN *closes her eyes, her body tilts, she moves her hands in the air.*)

MOLLY: Simple everyday activities. Reading a newspaper. Washing their hands. Very gentle. Not looking at each other. Saying those devastating words like there's nothing in them, this background music flowing out of their mouths, there's a helpless feeling, they're disconnected from what they're saying. Maybe a hand comes up, somebody grabs somebody, a moment of physical something, they're sort of touching but it makes no difference, they've gotten to this place they can't get back from and the soft voices just keep going, those hopeless words just keep pouring out of their heads. What do you think?

(ELLEN *opens her eyes, nods rapidly.*)

MOLLY: Great. And if that doesn't work we'll try something else.

6.

(ELLEN *sits on the floor, hugging her knees, rocking.* MOLLY *sits nearby.*)

MOLLY: This isn't what you want. Not really. You know that. Ellen? So can we tell Tom you changed your mind?

(ELLEN *keeps rocking.*)

MOLLY: You're afraid they'll see right through you, right? They'll see your insides on that stage, and what they'll see up there is shit, your stinking nauseating shit, they'll all point and laugh at this disgusting loser made of shit.

(ELLEN *nods.*)

MOLLY: Every playwright feels that way the night before an opening. So of course you want to cancel the play and crawl into a hole. But it's not fair to the actors, or to you. We've come so far, Ellen.

(ELLEN *keeps rocking.*)

MOLLY: Remember how you felt yesterday at the run through, when Ed and Abby really relaxed and made the lines their own? and started making all those great discoveries? it was scary and funny in a whole new way?

ELLEN: *(Still rocking)* Mm.

MOLLY: Something was alive. This new thing. Like nothing else that ever was. And it was yours. You made it.

ELLEN: Mm.

MOLLY: You felt tall.

ELLEN: Mmm.

MOLLY: Strong.

ELLEN: Mm.

MOLLY: Beautiful.

ELLEN: Mmmm.

MOLLY: Like you were flying.

(ELLEN *nods.*)

MOLLY: You could die and it would be completely fine.

(ELLEN *covers her eyes, stops rocking.*)

MOLLY: You can see any play as shit, Ellen. Because they're made by humans, these ridiculous flawed creatures who are all going to fall apart and stink. But wouldn't you rather believe in the work and have that tall feeling?

(ELLEN *nods.*)

MOLLY: So we'll tell Tom it's back on. You'll get some sleep, get some extra medication if you need it. And tomorrow you'll sit in back with me and watch everybody discover this incredible thing.

(ELLEN *nods, struggles to smile, sits up, smiles.*)

MOLLY: I love you Ellen. I love you so much it feels like my heart is going to explode. I don't know what to do with all this love.

(MOLLY *moves towards* ELLEN, ELLEN *backs off.*)

MOLLY: What I meant was, I love your play. That's what you want, right?

(ELLEN *nods.*)

MOLLY: I get confused sometimes, it happens. When Tom called I'd been drinking. There's stuff going on in my life. But I need you to understand that all the good things I said about the play I really meant. Okay Ellen?

(ELLEN *nods.*)

MOLLY: Good. So we're clear. It's all about the play.

7.

(MOLLY sits. ELLEN sits, a palm on her cheek.)

MOLLY: Everybody sits there, in the dark, in their own private space. Maybe they're totally into it. Or maybe it's not what they expected, so they're a little restless, but they're still taking it in. Over the next few days they replay it in their minds. It starts to feel more comfortable, reminds them of things they're going through, might even stir up all these associations and feelings and become a part of their whole sense of what it's like to be on earth. Or not. But in the moment, sitting there in the dark, no one can possibly know what they're feeling. Well I guess we know the ones who walked out weren't engaged in the way we hoped. Really though, when people walk out that just means they're not right for the piece, so by leaving they improve the quality of your audience. And if you're upset that the people from the Rep didn't come that's not about you, the play I've been directing for them isn't going well, they couldn't blame the actors, they're in the company, they couldn't blame the playwright, he's a name, so the problem had to be that I'm bad, and nobody wants to associate with somebody who's bad so my friends didn't come. Fuck it. The point is, a couple people said nice things about your play but they didn't really love it like they should have. So what. You know it's good Ellen. Don't start doubting yourself, you can't go down that road. I'm not crazy, I know what I know, and I sat there feeling so proud of what we'd done, loving it more than ever, thinking what's wrong with these people, they should be laughing and cheering and stomping til the ground shakes, this is a gem it's a masterpiece. Okay? So what the hell. (Taking out cookies) Let's have some cookies.

(ELLEN gets up, goes.)

MOLLY: Ellen?

8.

(MOLLY *reclines, eyes closed, speaks in a different tone.*
ELLEN *stands.*)

MOLLY: "Someone from the House" they said. Which
house. My mom's already here. My son too. "Harbor
House" they said. Ellen. I'm not opening my eyes
because there's a black shape that keeps expanding.
It's annoying but not scary. I'm on more medications
than you. I can't move my legs but at least they let me
keep them. As you go along in life you lose everything.
But you gain something. The knowledge of how it feels
to lose everything. I've been working through things
in my mind. But there's one thing I can't get my mind
around. The night we did your play. It was so great
in readings. But when we did it, it didn't work. The
problem was the space. We shouldn't have done it
outside. That play needs a closed space. So people can
focus. It got lost outside. We should have stayed in the
basement. It crossed my mind during rehearsals. But
I didn't say anything. Why didn't I say anything. And
we should have used a real table from the common
room. Tom had us use a bridge table. It never felt real.
The table was our main set piece. It had to be real. It
felt fake. A bridge table. I should have just said no.
This was five years ago. I can't get my mind around it.
I tried to visit you. They said you didn't want visitors.
I couldn't stand the thought of you still sitting by
yourself at meals. Hunched over all the time. Like
you don't deserve to live. When you walk into a room
people should cheer. Because you're a genius. Like
nobody who ever lived. Everyone should know that.
They don't even know your name. And it's my fault.

You trusted me with your play and I blew it. I'm sorry
Ellen.

(ELLEN *reaches into her clothes, takes out pieces of paper
folded together.*)

MOLLY: I know that sound. You wrote another play.
Can I read it.

(ELLEN *puts the script in* MOLLY's *hand, helps her bring it
close to her face.* MOLLY *opens her eyes, reads.*)

MOLLY: You gave the characters names this time.

(ELLEN *watches as* MOLLY *reads.*)

MOLLY: (*Closes her eyes*) I'll have to get back to it.
(*Moves hand and script away*) But right from the
beginning, I know that conversation. And I know the
people. It's you and me.

(ELLEN *nods.*)

MOLLY: You captured the feeling of how we
communicate. It's us. But it's every collaboration.
People working together on something they love.

(ELLEN *nods.*)

MOLLY: So after the last play you got right to work on
the next one.

(ELLEN *nods.*)

MOLLY: I was trying to explain the audience response.
You were having a new idea.

(ELLEN *nods.*)

MOLLY: That's why you didn't want visitors.

(ELLEN *nods.*)

MOLLY: You weren't mad at me.

(ELLEN *shakes her head.*)

MOLLY: You were busy with the next play.

(ELLEN *nods.*)

MOLLY: You had to figure it out. And get it right. So you could bring it to me.

(ELLEN *nods.*)

MOLLY: You were right, Ellen. The last play doesn't matter. It's done. Let it go. All that matters is the next one. You just keep going.

(ELLEN *nods.*)

MOLLY: We have to do this play. We'll get more experienced actors this time. I've been talking with the new guy at the Rep. He's better than the last guy. I'll submit it for his new play festival.

(ELLEN *stands there.*)

MOLLY: It's not finished is it. When you heard about me Tom rushed you over.

(ELLEN *nods.*)

MOLLY: That's okay. You can revise it during rehearsals. They've got a great space. New seats for you to hide behind.

(ELLEN *stands there.*)

MOLLY: I'm coming to a transition, Ellen. Like with the tornado. We were heading towards one kind of production. Then we shifted to another kind. After this transition you'll still hear me. You've always heard me. And I've always heard you. We'll keep right on working together. We'll get this play right. And the next one and the next one. And people will see our plays. And love our plays. And be inspired to make their plays. We'll all be making plays together. Always. Turning our feelings into characters. Putting our pieces out there. Adding them to the one big masterpiece, the whole story of being human, that we're sending into space. My name won't be on it. But my heart will be in it. And so will yours.

(ELLEN *trembles, takes* MOLLY's *hand, kisses it, pats* MOLLY's *hair, touches her cheek, her arm, kisses her, holds her.)*

MOLLY: I love working with you Ellen. There are so many kinds of love. But the best is the love you share with a collaborator. Someone you can communicate with. Complete honesty. Total understanding. How amazing it is. That we can find a way to express ourselves. That we can move each other. Make each other laugh. Let's give ourselves a hand for that. Let's cheer. Ellen. Thank you for writing this play. I love your play. It feels so great to be working.

(ELLEN *dances with intensity, holding* MOLLY's *hand.)*

END OF PLAY